The writers of *Incantations* tell us, "We have made this book as we make our children, with the strength of our flesh and the birds of our heart."

Open this book. It's the same, familiar world, but seen differently. The lines in this book are like the courses of birds flying. Their precision comes not from control but from abandon. There are no contours, for everything is contiguous, everything touches, as do the feathers of tails and wings. This is a book to fly with.

John Berger

Ámbar Past and the Taller Leñateros are an exciting cross-cultural cooperative that has united Mayan artists and poets in a collective workshop in San Cristóbal de las Casas, Mexico, the heart of the Mayan highlands in Chiapas. They are at the forefront of the renaissance in Mayan culture in this region, nearly five centuries after the Franciscan friars burned the Mayas' immensely rich but "idolatrous" treasure lode of classical literature. This collective book of poems and incantations is unique because it represents a collaboration between one naturalized Mexican poet and more than a dozen or so unschooled and unpublished poets from several Mayan linguistic backgrounds. Many members of the workshop are women who sing of their joys and sorrows during a time of rapid social change: separation from their husbands sent to the exploitative labor camps in coffee country; the struggle to maintain cultural integrity in the face of globalization and neoliberalism; and the celebration of traditional sources of spiritual energy and solidarity.

Cynthia Steele
Politics, Gender, and the Mexican Novel, 1968-1988: Beyond the Pyramid

INCANTATIONS
SONGS, SPELLS AND IMAGES BY MAYAN WOMEN

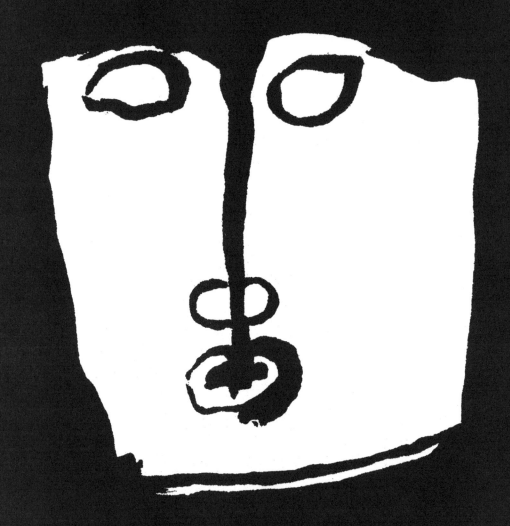

INCANTATIONS
SONG, SPELLS AND IMAGES BY MAYAN WOMEN

Fathermothers of the Book

ÁMBAR PAST

with

XALIK GUZMÁN BAKBOLOM
and XPETRA ERNANDES

Cinco Puntos Press  El Paso

Originally published in San Cristóbal, Chiapas, Mexico as *Incantations by Mayan Women*, a hand-made, hand-bound, limited edition by Taller Leñateros, 2005. Copyright © Ámbar Past, 2005.

FIRST EDITION
10 9 8 7 6 5 4 3 2 1

Library of Congress Cataloging-in-Publication Data

Conjuros y ebriedades. English
 Incantations: Songs, Spells and Images by Mayan women / by Ámbar Past with Xalik Guzmán Bakbolom and Xpetra Ernandes ; translated by Ámbar Past. — 1st ed.
    p. cm.
 Originally published: Chiapas, Mexico : Taller Leñateros, 2005.
 ISBN 1-933693-09-6
 1. Tzotzil poetry—Translations into English. 2. Tzotzil women. 3. Women shamans—Mexico—Chiapas. 4. Artists' books—Mexico—Chiapas. I. Past, Ambar. II. Guzmán Bakbolom, Xalik. III. Ernandes, Xpetra. IV. Title.

PM4466.Z95E533 2007
897.4287--dc22

                    2007000966

Cover illustration: Roselia Montoya

Book design: J.B. Bryan
(with a close and admiring eye on the original work of Ámbar Past and the Taller Leñateros.)

In the womb of my mother
I learned the spells.

In the womb of my mother
I heard them.

I took the basket,
I received the bottle,
I was given incense,
I was shown the Book.

From the womb of my mother,
I dreamed the incantations.

—*Pasakwala Kómes*

TABLE OF CONTENTS

In the Womb of My Mother I Learned the Spells   *Pasakwala Kómes*   *7*

Prayer   *Xpétra Ernándes*   *18*

Introduction to the English Edition   *Ámbar Past*   *19*

Who Is Its Mother?   *Ritual de los Bacabes*   *28*

She of the Great Writing, She of the Glyphs
an Introduction to Mayan Culture and Poetics   *Ámbar Past*   *29*

Fragments of Song Within the Essay:

From Learning to Dye Wool   *María Tzu*

From To the Bearer of Time   *Manwela Kokoroch*

From The Discovery and Conquest of Mexico   *Bernal Díaz de Castillo*

From Relación de las Cosas de Yucatan   *Friar Diego de Landa*

Words Grow Out of the Heart   *Munda Tostón*

The Seer Comes Singing   *Munda Tostón*

From For a Frightened Child Who Cannot Sleep   *Petú Bak Bolom*

Calling the Soul   *María Tzu*

From For Maruch Vet, Sold to a Cave   *Antel Péres Ck'il*

From So the Corn Will Last for Awhile   *María Tzu*

Talking Stone, Talking Tree   *Ritual de los Bacabes*

From Historia de la Provincia de Chiapas   *Fray Francisco Ximénez*

Note to the Talking Box   *Author unknown*

The Mother of Corn   *María Xila*

From To the Soul of Corn   *Xpetra Ernándes Jiménes*

The Mother of Fire   *María Tzu*

Earthquake Mother   *Munda Tostón*

Holy Snake   *Munda Tostón*

From To Stop the Mother Wind   *Petú Bak Bolom*

From Against the Rainbow   *María Tzu*

To Scare the *Pukuj*   *Xalik Guzmán Bakbolom*

From To *Kaxail*   *Maruch Méndes Péres*

From To Plant the Earth   *Jwana te la Krus Posol*

From Perils of the Soul   *Calixta Guiteras Holms*

A Potter's Song   *Beronika Uch*

From Before Felling a Tree   *Antonia Moshán Culej*

From So the New House Won't Eat Us   *Xunka' Utz'utz'Ni'*

A Story About Stalactites   *Maruch Méndes Péres*

From To *Kaxail*   *Maruch Méndes Péres*

From Song for Rain   *María Xila*

Suyul   *María Xila*

Weaving the First Shirt   *Petú Xantis*

From How the Moon Taught Us to Weave   *Loxa Jiménex Lópes*

Rebellion of the Cooking Pots   *Popol Vuh*

From For the Harp   *Xpetra Ernándes Jiménes*

From Ten Blues of the Sky   *Mikaela Moshán Culej*

From During the Eclipse   *Petú Xantis Xantis*

From To the Bearer of Time   *Manwela Kokoroch*

From The Discovery and Conquest of Mexico   *Bernal Diaz de Castillo*

From To Keep the Soldiers Away   *Xunka' Utz'utz' Ni'*

The Virgin Was trying to Find a Place to Live   *Me' Avrila*

The Virgin Speaks   *Loxa Jiménex*

Song of the Midwives of God   *Maria Patixtán Likán Chitom*

From A Midwife Addresses the Newborn   *Rosa Xulemhó*

From Witchcraft for Attracting a Man   *Xpetra Ernándes Jiménes*

From Lullaby   *Petra Tzon Te' Vitz*

To The Mother of the Most Difficult   *Munda Tostón*

From For a Dead Child   *Loxa Jiménex Lópes*

I am So Used to Not Being Dead   *Me' Avrila*

From Feeding the Black Dog   *Munda Tostón*

Mother of the Night   *Xalik Guzmán Bakbolom*

In Venustiano Carranza   *Guadalupe Domínguez*

The Penis Measuring Stone   *Munda Tostón*

I am Half Woman   *Antzil Ak'ot*

Sex Education Couplets   *Bankilal Ik'al*

From Dance of the Perfumed Woman   *Tonik Nibak*

To Cure Insanity   *Xunka' Utz'utz' Ni'*

A Potter's Song   *María Tzu*

Asking for Help   *Me' Avrila*

To End a Fight   *Xunka' Utz'utz' Ni'*

The Penis Song   *Maruch Méndes Péres*

Bolom Chon   *María Tzu*

From A Toast   *Mikaela Moshán Culej*

From Prayer So My Man Won't Have to Cross the Line   *Xunka' Utz'utz' Ni'*

Through Writing We Know   *Ritual de los Bacabes*

The First Fathermother   *Temple of the Cross, Palenque*

The Corresponding Glyphs   *Ritual de los Bacabes*

The Language of *Zuyya*   *Books of Chilam Balan*

To The Grandmother of the Day   *Popol Vuh*

From Antología de Poesía Primitiva   *Ernesto Cárdenal*

From Technicians of the Sacred   *Jerome Rothenberg*

To The Elder Brother of Writing   *Manwela Kokoroch*

The Incantations

I am a Woman My Woman   *Loxa Jiménes Lópes*   93

The Bonesetter's Song   *Pasakwala Kómes*   96

So the Bat Won't Bite the Sheep   *María Tzu*   97

The Mother of Treasure   *Xunka' Utz'utz' Ni'*   100

To *Kaxail*   *Maruch Méndes Péres*   101

Planting a Tree   *Xpetra Ernándes Jiménes*   102

Witchcraft for Attracting a Man   *Xpetra Ernándes Jiménes*   103

So the Dog Won't Bark at My Boyfriend   *Xpetra Ernándes Jiménes*   104

To Plant the Earth   *Jwana te la Krus Posol*   107

To the Blue Jay   *Antonia Moshán Culej*   108

Prayer So My Man Won't Have to Cross the Line   *Xunka' Utz'utz' Ni'*   110

Song for Rain   *María Xila*   111

Against the Rainbow   *María Tzu*   114

Words to Bring Down Fever   *Pasakwala Kómes*   117

For the Harp   *Xpetra Ernándes*   118

The Saint Keepers' Song   *María Patixtán Likán Chitom*   119

The Bolom Chon   *Rominka Vet*   120

A Toast   *Mikaela Moshán Culej*   121

The Drunken Woman's Song   *Maruch Méndes Péres*   124

Calling the Dead to Supper   *María Álvares Jímenes, Me' Avrila*   127

How the Moon Taught Us to Weave   *Loxa Jiménes Lópes*   128

To Enchant the Spindle   *Xpetra Ernándes Jiménes*   129

Learning to Dye Wool   *María Tzu*   130

A Girl's Song About a Tangled Loom   *María Patixtán Likán Chitom*   132

Asking for Her Hand   *Markarita Váskes Kómes*   135

Before Felling a Tree   *Antonia Moshán Culej*   136

To the Wildwood   *Xpetra Ernándes Jiménes*   137

So the New House Won't Eat Us   *Xunka' Utz'utz' Ni'*   138

Borrowing a Gourd   *María Álvares Jímenes, Me' Avrila*   140

To Return a Ceremonial Huipil   *María Álvares Jímenes, Me' Avrila*   141

Against the Hummingbird Who Sings at Night   *María Tzu*   144

During the Eclipse   *Petú Xantis Xantis*   145

A Midwife Addresses the Newborn   *Rosa Xulemhó*   146

Lullaby   *Petra Tzon Te Vitz*   149

For a Frightened Child Who Cannot Sleep   *Petú Bak Bolom*   150

For a Dead Child   *Loxa Jiménes Lópes*   151

So the Baby will Learn to Speak   *Antonia Moshán Culej*   152

A Girl's Song about a Wild Deer   *Verónika Taki Vaj*   153

Song of a Shepherdess   *María Patixtán Likán Chitom*   156

To Stop Mother Wind   *Petú Bak Bolom*   157

For Maruch Vet, Sold to a Cave   *Antel Péres Ok'il*   158

Drinking with the Dead   *María Álvares Jímenes, Me' Avrila*   161

So the Lizard Won't Eat the Beans   *María Tzu*   162

To the Soul of Corn   *Xpetra Ernándes Jiménes*   163

So the Corn Will Last for Awhile   *María Tzu*   166

To Keep the Soldiers Away   *Xunka' Utz'utz' Ni'*   167

Ten Blues of the Sky   *Mikaela Moshán Culej*   168

So I Won't Have to Steal   *Loxa Jiménes Lópes*   171

Pexi Kola Magic   *Loxa Jiménes Lópes*   172

The Talking Box   *María Ernándes Kokov*   173

Potzlom   *Manwela Kokoroch*   174

Potzlom   *María Patixtán Likán Chitom*   175

Drinking Again   *Maruch Méndes Péres*   178

Song of the Plumed Serpent   *Loxa Jiménes Lópes*   179

The Woman With a Mask of Earth   *María Kartones*   180

The *Xpakinté*   *Munda Tostón*   181

Hex to Kill the Unfaithful Man   *Tonik Nibak*   184

To the Bearer of Time   *Manwela Kokoroch*   185

Feeding the Black Dog   *Munda Tostón*   189

A Wake   *Maruch Méndes Péres*   190

A Drinking Song by the Wife of the *Alperez*   *Pawakwala Kómes*   191

Dance of the Perfumed Woman   *Tonik Nibak*   192

Notes on the Creators   *Ámbar Past*   195

Notes on *Incantations by Mayan Women*   *Ámbar Past*   219

Bibliography   223

ORIGINAL SILKSCREEN GRAPHICS

Mother of the Book   Roselia Montoya 2

Woman Dancing   Mikaela Días Días 8

The Suns   María Tzu 14

Painter   Sluz Hernándes 17

The Moon is Dancing   Mikaela Días Días 22 & 23

Woman Dreaming   Rosa Lópes Kómes 27

The Seer   Petrona Ruiz 33

Woman Making Tortillas   Sluz Hernándes 41

Xpakinté   Rosa Lópes Kómes 42

Pukuj Rainbow   Petrona Ruiz 47

Pukuj   Petrona Ruiz 48

Suyl   Salvador Guzmán 60

Weaving   María Patixtán Likán Chitcom 63

Altar   María Tzu 64

Drunken Women   Mikaela Días Días 72 & 73

A River of Blood   María Tzu 78

We Will Shake Him Three Times   María Tzu 83

Rituals   María Tzu 84

Musicians   Sluz Hernándes 88

Dwarf in the Underworld   Loxa Jiménes Lópes 90

The Conjure Woman   Sluz Hernándes 88

Bats Attacking the Sheep   Mikaela Días Días 98 & 99

Women Breaking the Face of the Earth   Manwela Kómes Kómes 105

Working the Cornfield   Loxa Jiménes Lópes 106

Mother of Hail   Mikaela Días Días 112 & 113

Curing the Fever with Thirteen Flowers   Manwela Kómes Kómes 115

I Am Nine Pine Buds   Mikaela Días Días 116

Two Women Drinking   Sluz Hernándes 122 & 123

Supper for the Dead   Xunka' Utz'ut' Ni' 125

Feast for the Dead   *Laura Peale   126*

Woman in the Flower   *María Tzu   133*

Face of the Sun in Eclipse   *Jasinto Lópes Lópes   134*

The Night Hummingbird   *Marselino Patixtán   142 & 143*

Women Giving Birth   *María Tzu   147*

Man with No Face   *Loxa Jiménes Lópes   148*

For a Frightened Girl Who Cannot Sleep   *Loxa Jiménes Lópes   154 & 155*

Maruch Vet, Sold to a Cave   *Jasinto Lópes Lópes   159*

Shamans Doing Magic   *María Tzu   160*

Mothers of Corn   *Estela Hernández Téllez   164 & 165*

Maruch Vet within the Hill   *Rosa Lópes Kómes   169*

Mother of Wind Has a Red Heart   *Loxa Jiménes Lópes   170*

Two Storytellers   *Sluz Hernándes   176 & 177*

Talking Boxes   *María Tzu   182 & 183*

Black Dog Eating its Tortilla   *Mikaela Días Días   188 & 189*

Woman with the Mask of Earth   *Mikaela Días Días   193*

Maria Kartones   *Mikaela Días Días   194*

A Wake   *Marselino Patixtán   206*

Red *Potzlam*   *Loxa Jiménes Lópes   209*

Black *Potzlam*   *Loxa Jiménes Lópes   210*

Envious Woman Provoking an Eclipse of the Sun and the Moon   *Maria Tzu   218*

Toadstool Woman   *Mikaela Días Días   230*

Prayer

We are happy, sacred paper,
sacred book,

sacred words,
sacred paintings.

You've come out in another language
called English,

the tongue of the white folks
who have blonde hair.

Don't scold us, book,
be of one heart,
sing and dance,

because you are going to travel far away
to another land.

—*Xpetra Ernándes*

INTRODUCTION

to the English edition of *Incantations: Songs, Spells and Images by Mayan Women*

THE TZOTZIL-SPANISH EDITION OF THIS BOOK, *Conjuros y ebriedades*, came to light in 1998, the culmination of twenty-three years of work. It was the very first iteration of what would later become the fuller *Incantations* in Tzotzil and English, from which the book you're holding in your hands—the U.S. edition—was eventually born.

Conjuros y ebriedades was formally presented in the Tamayo Museum in Mexico City with the participation of eighteen of the Mayan authors, two drummers, and a flautist from Huixtán. We took the twenty-hour bus ride to Mexico City, lugging nets of pine needles to spread on the stage and in the aisles, and broke all the fire department's rules, filling the darkened auditorium with glowing candles and Mayan incense.

María Tzu, Loxa Jiménes, Xpetra Ernándes, Maruch Méndez, her tiny Xvel, Mikaela Días Días, Xunká Utz'utz' Ni', María Patixtán Likán Chitom, Sluz Hernández, and Mikaela and Antonia Moshán Culej sipped *pox* and sang as though they were quite accustomed to performing for a thousand people. Much of the public was moved to tears by the women's incantations. Spanish television filmed the event, as did the cultural channel of Mexico. Subcomandante Marcos congratulated our efforts with a note in his own hand:

> Here we have our own incantations.
> And even though drinking is not allowed,
> We have our drunken songs.
> We sing, not only of suffering and injustice,
> But also just because it's morning.
> Especially in the morning.
> That's when we sing.
> —*Subcomandante Marcos*

A big photo of our book presentation dominated the front page of *La Jornada*, Mexico's leading newspaper, and our work was applauded in all the other papers as well. We celebrated by climbing the Pyramids of the Sun and the Moon. Actress Angéla Aragón took us to see the Voladores de Papantla, Amerindian acrobats who perform atop a sort of telephone pole they erect in Chapultepec Park. They shimmied up and then, tying themselves on by their ankles to a rickety merry-go-round high above us, they dove off and spun head down while a fellow played the flute and drum way up in the sky.

We visited the shrine of the Virgin of Guadalupe, and even though María Tzu is now a Protestant, she was captivated by the electric sidewalk that circles around the Virgin. Along with Loxa, Maruch, and Xvel, she rode the magic path again and again, overwhelmed with Our Lady's technology. We took in kilometers of murals by Diego Rivera and the wondrous Museum of the Templo Mayor of Tenochtitlan. We saw all the sights.

Actually our group was quite a sight in itself as we walked around downtown. The musicians brought along their drums which had been carved out of tree trunks. The drummers wore what they call pants, but what look to me like raggedy hand-woven diapers, barely covering their very muscular thighs. Brightly colored ribbons streamed down from their flat pizza-pan straw hats. Decked out in their best *huipils*, the seers were dressed to kill. Xpetra has hair down to her knees and she had braided it very coquettishly with red yarn pompons. Maruch's little girl was wearing her woolly black skirt, crimson sash, and turquoise blue blouse. Everyone was laughing, it was a beautiful day!

When we got to the museum, they just let us in. The guards didn't ask for tickets or anything. I assumed the role of Tzotzil tour guide at first, commenting that the Great Temple had been an important church for the First Fathermothers *blah blah*. Just inside the door we stumbled upon a ritual pile of skulls and I stammered a bit about human sacrifice, the taking out of the heart. The Tzotzils took it a lot better than I thought they would. How would you feel if you found out your great-great-grandmother had been a cannibal, or that she kept slaves and took part in "satanic rites"?

We were admiring some ancient ceramic dishes that had been pierced in the center—"killed" was the explanation an archeologist had once given me. Just as I was about to open my mouth again to "explain," I heard Xpetra telling María Tzu in Tzotzil that the plates had been sacrificed, that their hearts had been taken out.

The drummers became very animated when they recognized the planet Venus on an Aztec stone sculpture of the heavens. *The Fathermothers could see the same stars as we can!* they cried out and everyone in the museum ran over to admire their discovery. A couple of tourists asked if THEY, pointing to the Mayans, were "part of the exhibit."

We sold 1,500 copies of *Conjuros* faster than even our wildest dreams. Many copies of our handmade book were purchased by university libraries. We paid royalties to the authors of the incantations, to the painters who created the graphics, and also to the artisans who molded the mask covers and printed and bound the texts and the forty-four original silk screens.

The overwhelmingly positive response to our work inspired us to translate the original book into Italian, French, and English. The number of new texts in the anthology snowballed along with the enthusiasm and self-esteem of the authors. The celebration of 500 years of Indian resistance and the Zapatista uprising has fostered an ever-growing appreciation for the art and literature of Native Peoples. We found ourselves immersed in a reawakening of the spirit of Amerindian culture.

Maruch Méndes Péres has learned many new songs and Rosa Xulemhó has offered to share with us her incantations for midwifery. Mikaela Moshán Culej and her sister Antonia Moshán Culez from Chilil have participated as part of the Leñateros team for many years, insisting they knew no incantations, but when Mikaela's son Evodio died, she began to sing, and her sister Antonia came to remember poems long forgotten. Xpetra Ernándes began to write on the computer, and is typing up her own incantations.

Finally, Xalik Guzmán Bakbolom (alias Xun Okotz), who had originally disguised himself, has given permission for his real name to be used in the credits as one of the Fathermothers of the Book.

I had always hoped that Cinco Puntos Press would create a trade edition of *Incantations* and this is now a dream come true, thanks to the magic of Lee and Bobby Byrd.

These are inspiring times for the Maya. In 2001, the Zapatista Caravan, the "March of the Color of the Earth," grabbed our souls and hearts, taking us all over Mexico on a mission to address Congress about Amerindian rights. Twenty-four Mayan *comandantes* and a cosmopolitan entourage filling more than a hundred busses toured the country for almost a month. Multitudes turned out to receive the Caravan wherever it went. Men and women and school children dressed in white gathered in the plazas of the cities and towns. They waited for hours along the highways waving sugarcanes, they hung off bridges, holding up banners and hand-lettered signs of support for Amerindian rights.

When the Zapatistas arrived in Nurío, Michoacán, where the National Indian Congress was being held, Tzotziles, Huichols, Ñames, Tarahumaras, and delegates from more than fifty ethnic groups joined the Caravan to demand that the San Andrés Accords, signed by the Mexican government and the Zapatistas in 1995, finally be honored.

Amerindian women from the whole continent linked arms to protect the comandantes along the route. In Milpa Alta, the Nahuatl community paid for and prepared with their own hands—using corn they grew themselves—breakfast, lunch, and dinner for 30,000 during three days and nights. In downtown Mexico City, hundreds of thousands shouted *"Long live indigenous women!"*

As the culmination of the Caravan, a Tzotzil Mayan woman, Comandanta Esther, was chosen by the Zapatistas to address Congress; her speech sent chills of emotion down our spines.

My name is Esther, but that is not important now. I am a Zapatista, but that is not important at this moment either.

Deputies, Ladies and Gentlemen. Senators. I would like to explain to you the situation of the indigenous women who are living in our communities, considering that respect for women is supposedly guaranteed in the Constitution. Our situation is very difficult. For many years we have suffered pain, neglect, contempt, marginalization, and oppression. We suffer because no one remembers that we exist. We have been forgotten in the remote mountains of the country; no one comes to visit us or sees how we are living. We do not have drinkable water, electricity, school, adequate housing, roads, clinics—let alone hospitals. Many of our sisters, women, children and the old die from curable diseases, malnutrition and childbirth, because there is no place where they can be treated.

It is the women who feel the pain of childbirth. We watch our children die in our arms from malnutrition, from lack of care. Our children run barefoot and naked because we do not have money to buy shoes and clothing. We do not have enough food to eat, and are obliged to walk two or three hours to fetch water and firewood. We carry huge burdens on tumplines, and also do all the child care and kitchen work. From the time we are very young, we begin doing chores. When we are bigger, we go to work in the fields, we plant, weed, carrying our children on our backs.

24

Meanwhile, the men go off to work in the coffee plantations and cane fields to earn a little money for their families. Sometimes they do not come home again, or they come back sick, with no money, sometimes already dead. And so the woman is left with more pain, she is left alone caring for her children.

From the moment we are born we suffer from contempt and marginalization, because no one looks out for our interests. Because we are females, they do not think we are worth anything. They believe we do not know how to think or how to live our lives. That is why many of us women are illiterate, because we did not have the opportunity to go to school.

When we are a bit older, our fathers force us to marry. It does not matter if we do not want to, they do not ask for our consent. They abuse our decisions. They beat us, we are mistreated by our own husbands and their relatives. We cannot say anything because they tell us we do not have a right to defend ourselves. The mestizos and the wealthy mock us indigenous women because of our way of dressing, of speaking, our language, our way of praying and of curing, and for our color, which is the color of the earth we work.

We, the indigenous women, do not have the same opportunities as the men who decide everything. Only they have the right to the land; women do not have rights since we are not human beings.

This is the way of life and death for us indigenous women. This is why we decided to organize ourselves to fight as Zapatista women, in order to change the situation. We are tired of so much suffering, we are tired of not having our rights. I am not telling you all this so you will pity us or come to save us from these abuses. We have struggled to change the situation, and we will continue to do so. First off we need to be recognized as human beings. This is where we need to start. We are the lowest of the low; the indigenous woman is the most exploited of an exploited society.

Some of our traditions are intolerable, including hitting and beating women, buying and selling us, forcing us to marry against our will, denying our participation in assembly, locking us up in our homes.

These are some of the reasons why we want the San Andrés Accords to be implemented. It is very important for us, for the indigenous women of all of Mexico.

The San Andrés Accords will make it possible for us to be recognized and respected as human beings.

We want our way of dress recognized, our way of speaking, of governing, of organizing, of praying, of curing, our method of working in collectives, of respecting the land and of understanding life, which is nature, of which we are a part. Our rights as women are also defined by this law. Now no one will be able to limit our participation, our dignity, and our safety in any kind of work will be assured. We will have the same rights as men.

That is why we want to remind all the Deputies and Senators to carry out their duties as true representatives of the people. Do not allow anyone to put our dignity to shame any longer.

Many years have passed since Comandanta Esther addressed Congress in Tzotzil Maya, and the government has still not responded to the basic human needs she enumerates in her speech. The San Andrés Accords have yet to be signed by the government. Years after the Acteal massacre of 45 Tzotzil Mayans—most of whom were women and children—the perpetrators of this barbarous act are still at large. How many women must be killed in the world before we begin to hear their voices?

—Ámbar Past

Who is its mother?
Glyphs of the skies.
Glyphs of the clouds.

Who is its mother?
And it is said,
Ix Hun Tah Dzib, She of the Great Writing,
Ix Hun Uooh, She of the Glyphs.

The corresponding glyphs
that were together,
separated
and so acquired
incantations
from saliva.

—Ritual de los Bacabes

SHE OF THE GREAT WRITING,
SHE OF THE GLYPHS

An Introduction to Mayan Culture and Poetics :: *Ámbar Past*

THESE INCANTATIONS were dreamed by Mayan women in the Highlands of Chiapas in southern Mexico. The Tzotzil authors of this anthology claim their spells and songs were given to them by the ancestors, the First Fathermothers, who keep the Great Book in which all words are written down. Pasakwala Kómes, an unlettered seer from Santiago El Pinar, learned her conjurations by dreaming the Book. Loxa Jimenés Lópes of Epal Ch'en, Chamula, tells of an *Anjel*, daughter of the Lord of the Caves, who began whispering in her ear and then, in dreams, showed her the Book with all the magic words to be learned.

> Show me your three books,
> your three letters,
> the ink of the letters,

prays María Tzu to ask for the secret of black dye, directing her verses to the Ancient Earth in Flower, the Coffer Where the Secrets Are Kept.

Manwela Kokoroch, from Laguna Petej, Chamula, sings to the Elder Brothers of Writing and Painting, who hold the Book where the names of all the people in the world are written down, along with the dates of their deaths. Here she pleads for a long life:

> Let my animal spirit live
> many more years
> in the pages of the Book,
> in its letters,
> its paintings,
> on the whole surface of the Earth.

Even though few of the authors of this anthology can read, even though the Tzotzil Maya have no libraries nor bookstores near their houses, a wise person is said to have "books in the heart," according to Robert M. Laughlin's translation of a sixteenth-century Spanish-Tzotzil dictionary.

The Mayan word for book, *jun* or *vun*, also means paper, and the making of paper is an important Mesoamerican tradition. During rituals, ancient Mayan women pierced their tongues and dripped the blood on paper which was then burnt. Even today in the *amate* papermaking town of San Pablito Pahuatlán in Puebla, paper is still burnt as an offering to the gods.

In Tzotzil, to write and to paint are the same verb *(tz'ib)*, just as the color *yox* serves for what English speakers perceive as both blue and green. Antonia Moshán Culej of Huixtán asks: "How is it that María Tzu can paint if she can't write?" Weaving is today considered to be a form of script and Tzotzil women can read the verses on their looms.

The ancient Mayan god Itzamná is credited with the invention of writing. His wife is said to have created the universe by painting everything into existence. The Fathermothers gave birth to one of the few civilizations in the world that conceived a way to write down its language. The ancestors of Loxa Jiménes, María Tzu, and Manwela Kokoroch created the Mayan codices, magnificent books written when only Native People inhabited these lands. On stuccoed bark paper pages, they painted forecasts of the movements of the heavenly bodies, prophesies, divinations, and spells. In his chronicle *The Conquest of New Spain*, Bernal Díaz de Castillo, a soldier who accompanied Cortes in the invasion of Mexico, wrote:

> We found temples and places of sacrifice, and blood splashed about, and the incense they burnt, and other properties of their idols, also the stones on which they made their sacrifices, and parrots' feathers, and many of their books, which are folded as cloth is in Spain.

The Maya seems to hold ancient memories of their libraries. Even today, the oral poetry of ritual speech is referred to as *tz'ib*, "that which is painted or written down." Poetry is called *nichimal k'op*, "the word in flower." We know of only four pre-Columbian Mayan books that survived the ravages of time and war; many were destroyed by Friar Diego de Landa in the sixteenth century, as documented in his *Relación de las cosas de Yucatan*:

> [The Maya] wrote their books on a long sheet of paper doubled in pleats, the whole thing enclosed between two boards that made them very attractive...

There were many beautiful books, but as they contained nothing but superstitions and falsehoods of the Devil, we burnt them all, and this affected [the Maya] deeply, causing them great sorrow and grief.

Song is a book that will not burn. In the early colonial period, a number of ancient Mayan texts were transcribed in Latin characters and translated into Spanish. The best known of these is the *Popol Vuh*—the sacred book of the K'iché. The Yucatec Maya conserved their magical writings in the *Books of Chilam Balam, the Codex of Calkiní* and—perhaps the most exquisite poetry left us by the ancient Maya—a volume of incantations entitled the *Ritual de los Bacabes*.

It is clear the First Fathermothers were writers, and it is rumored that some of their books—that no one can read anymore—lie hidden in old chests in Chamula. Each year they are taken out with great reverence, perfumed with incense and wrapped up again in embroidered cloths. Some say the books inside the chests have begun to talk. Women who learn the words are said to have writing in their hearts.

*Incantations by Mayan Women** is the first book Mayan people have created, written, illustrated, printed and bound—in paper of their own making—in nearly five hundred years.

TUESDAY is the best day for curing a woman. The *h-ilol*, which means "seer," cures her patient before an altar of sacred plants and candles in a cloud of *copal* incense. Her prayers may take all night.

> The words grow out of the heart
> and flow along the ways
> of our lifeblood.
> —*Munda Tostón*

If the sickness is very serious, the ceremony may go on for three days. The patient lies in a nest of flowers while the seer visits the holy places in caves and on mountain tops, offering sacred songs to the Fathermothers.

* This statement refers to the original handmade, handbound, limited edition of *Incantations by Mayan Women*, made by the Taller Leñateros in 2005.

The seer comes singing
and finds the word,
the caress of the word
inside the veins.
        —*Munda Tostón*

The word comes from the mouth of the seer. It lives a life of its own in the body of a snake. The word is larva that penetrates the Earth, emerges from the caves, flies through the air to fall as rain, sprinkling our bodies. The word penetrates the veins and the seer feels it in the pulse of the sick person. Words take the forms of stars, of circles, of glyphs drawn on the face of the blood.

The conjurer massages the patient with her song. The words form a ball of fire that challenges the hex of an enemy. The seer takes hold of the words of a witch and turns them against her so she wounds herself with the spell she meant for another.

We become ill when our soul is stolen from our body, or when we fall down and are frightened. The conjuress calls to the soul to come back, whistling to it on a little gourd.

Bring her back
with pine cones,
with wild berries,
and candles of many colors.
Let her come with her flowers blooming,
with flowers in her body,
Holy Mother Breast,
Sacred Earth,
Holy Wildwood.
        —*Petú Bak Bolom*

Children run the risk of losing their souls in places they don't know. Twenty years ago, when María Tzu, her baby Mateo, and I went to Mexico City, at every moment María called and shepherded the spirit of her child through the labyrinth of the subway.

Mateo, Mateo, come home,
come back to your body.
Come back, Mateo, to your mama.
Back to your clothes.
Back to your diaper.
Don't be afraid of the roads.
Don't be frightened by the cars.
Don't let your soul become tangled up
in the hand of the *Anjel Diablo.*
— *María Tzu*

In addition to her soul, each person has an animal companion called a *wayhel*, a word grown from the root (*way*) of the verbs *to sleep* and *to dream*, and associated with shamanism, the portals to the Underworld, communication with the gods and the dead. The *wayhel* accompanies its alter ego from the moment it is born and may be a jaguar, a hawk, a hummingbird, a butterfly, a weasel, a caterpillar, or a water snake.

Instead of a head, it may have an ax, a machete, a pair of scissors or even a cast-iron skillet stuck on the end of its neck. Witches may possess several *wayhel*: whirlwinds, rainbows, lightning bolts, and shooting stars. One of the most powerful forms of *wayhel* is the Writer, the *Scribanó.* This kind of *wayhel* is immortal because even after death she can recreate herself through marks on a piece of paper, or, as Pedro Pitarch explains: "...they invent themselves, writing themselves into existence."

The soul companions live with the Fathermothers in the heart of the mountain, sitting on the thirteen levels of bleachers inside the Earth. There the *wayhel* have radios, jukeboxes, even computers and e-mail.

In dreams, the *wayhel* souls escape like naughty children and run around loose out in the woods. If anything happens to her *wayhel*, a person will become ill. In these times when men are blasting new roads with dynamite, the earth trembles and the *wayhel* are afraid and can even die. A bad person may capture a *wayhel* and sell it to the Lord of the Cave, as happened to poor Maruch Vet. The soul is held captive in the way prisoners of war were held in ancient Mayan times, chained or tied with ropes awaiting sacrifice. The *wayhel* loses its appetite and becomes ill; its owner also gets sick. The seer offers a black hen to the cave so it will give back the stolen *wayhel* before her patient dies.

> Mother of the Night,
> Father of the Night,
>
> Great Star of Venus,
> Mother Month, Mother Moon:
>
> Get up! Put on your best clothes.
> Let Maruch Vet's body
>
> out of where she's scared to death,
> sold to a cave, sold to a mountain.
> —*Antel Péres Ok'il*

The force of the word can cure or kill. Some words must never be uttered unless the intention is to do evil, for pronouncing the name of something calls it to life. Euphemisms are employed when touching certain powerful themes. The *wayhel*, for example, might be referred to as sheep, and the Fathermothers as shepherds. A person's true name is known only to her parents and the seer and is considered to be so powerful that a child intentionally named for another will be known as that person's substitute, and is thought to acquire characteristics of her namesake.

Envious people cause sickness through witchcraft and noxious spells they chant in caves at night. You have to be careful not to make your neighbor envious of your new house, of the corn you are harvesting or the tortilla you put in your mouth. This is not easy in these times in which Mayan people lack just about everything. "Or you starve to death or they kill you with their envy," as my friend María Gutierrez explains.

> How much will I harvest, *Kajval*?
> How many of your sunbeams?

How much of your body
will I put in my basket, Father?

Let no one take it from me.
Let no one want what I have.
—*María Tzu*

Dreams can provoke a sickness called *Potzlom*, a form of cancer that causes eclipses of the Sun. A witch converts herself into a nightmare animal, a jaguar or a ball of fire that falls from the sky, causing swelling of the body and bad tumors. *Potzlom* can be cured with women's urine and poetry.

Seers acquire their gift within the womb. Four-year-old girls play at being *h-iloles*, creating tiny altars in their yards where they cure their dolls. When the girls are a little older, they dream the Fathermothers make them a present of incense and sacred herbs. They are given a whistling gourd to call the souls, a shot glass, and candles of every color. "Take this," the Fathermothers say to them while they sleep, "this is for you." Every night they dream in couplets and in this way come to know the incantations for curing. The *h-iloles* dream they are shown the Great Book where all the spells are written down.

A witch dreams of snakes: she grabs one, she bites it, she swallows the snake meat and it crawls down her throat very slowly. That is where her force is born. If she has enemies, she thinks, "*I am going to hurt them before they hurt me.*" In Tzotzil, the witch is *ak'chamel*, "the giver of sickness." Witchcraft is practiced behind closed doors. If people find you out, they'll chop you up with a machete. A curer can denounce the witch she believes is hurting her patient, and if the person dies her family members have the right to take justice into their own hands. A man is supposed to kill his wife or his mother-in-law when he catches either of them witching.

A witch is also called the Mother of Sickness. Sometimes you come upon processions of men and women singing and laughing under the black star-studded sky as though they were on their way home from a party, the men playing their harps and the women walking behind carrying incense burners filled with *copal*. These are the Mothers of Sickness and they always seem to be very happy.

The most powerful seers among the Tzotzil are the *Me' Santo*, the Saint Mothers, who cure with the words of a singing gourd or a talking box. The tradition of this Maya ocacle is ancient. The goddess *Ixchel* spoke through a talking saint on the island of Cozumel long before Christ came to the Caribbean.

> Four are the head of *Acantún*, Talking Stone,
> Four are the head of *Acante'*, Talking Tree.
> —*Ritual de los Bacabes*

In 1711, Dominica Lópes, a Mayan woman from Chamula, discovered a Virgin in her cornfield. The Virgin was carved of wood and spoke through the voice of Dominica. In 1712, a young woman in Cancuc became the interpreter for the Virgin of Candelaria when she spoke to the Tzeltal Maya people. Her words, uttered from behind a curtain of straw in the name of the Virgin, incited an Indian rebellion with the participation of the soldiers of the Virgin, allied with four witches named Earthquake, Lightning, Flood, and Wind. Fray Francisco Ximénez describes this uprising in *Historia de la Provincia de San Vicente de Chiapas y Guatemala*:

> There was an Indian girl who had her coven of witches and she promised her following that they had naught to fear for they had power over the storms and the lightning that would strike down their enemies, and in this way the Indians came out of the mountain towns four hundred strong along with two old women from Yajalón and two young women from Tila and an old blind man from the same place who was called King of the Witches, and they came to a place called the Hill of Vaquitepeque...carried in chairs covered with mats. When they asked the witches why no miracle had happened, it was explained that their language was not as strong as it had once been; that words in Spanish had defeated their Mayan prayers even though they had prayed long into the night. Because of this defeat, their people called them liars, but even so, they kept the faith in their witches and the effectiveness of their spells, the last resort they had to free themselves from the Spanish.

During the Caste War in nineteenth-century Yucatan, wooden and stone crosses spoke to the Maya people in their own language, inciting rebellion. In 1867, the Chamula shepherdess Agustina Kómes Checheb found three stones fallen from the wind. The stones began to speak. She put them in a wooden box and their voice led the Indian autonomy movement called the War of Saint Rose. Even today the place where the people gathered to listen to the talking stones is called *El Baux* (The Box).

Some say the Maya originally learned to cure from talking boxes that told them secrets. Women hear voices even today. Six years ago a woman from Epal Ch'en dreamed a voice was talking inside her head. The voice asked for its box, saying, "Mama, you are getting married." It was a talking saint. The woman got married, but her husband walked out on her, left her with three children; he couldn't take it that she talked to saints. Lots of people came to pray, bringing incense and candles to consult the Saint about fevers, robberies, boundary lines. The box spoke: it could tell you the names of your enemies, it baptized babies, it found what had been lost. And so the civil authorities came and burnt it up, saying it wasn't right for a woman to be the Mother of the Saint; they tied her to an oak tree as punishment.

There are a great many Mothers of Saints in the Highlands of Chiapas today, and some of the "Mothers" are men, although the tradition was once female. The voice from the talking box of María Ernándes Kokov, a modern commercialized version of a Mayan oracle, was taped in 1996 during an eclipse of the Moon seen from her house up on Huitepec Mountain, in be-tween the antennas of Televisión Azteca and a traditional animistic shrine. The Saint, named Pagresito, "Little Daddy," spoke with a falsetto voice to his keeper, María Ernándes Kokov, who calls herself the Defender of the Angels. She takes care of the Saint, intercedes with Pagresito, pleading for the interests of those who consult her, and performs all sorts of cures at specialist rates. I saw a fifty-peso bill on the Saint's altar and next to it was a scrap of paper with this message written by one of the clients:

> Pagresitos:
> Please tell the manager
> of the Koka Kola plant,
> tell him in his heart,
> that his word better be good.

EVERYTHING ON EARTH HAS A MOTHER. The Mother of Blood is the heart; the Mother of Water is thunder; the Mother of Hand is the thumb. Mother of Lightning sends the rain; Mother of the Light is a hydroelectric dam.

Mother of Corn is a double ear of corn; you only find one or two in each cornfield. It looks like the body of a woman with long hair. When a Mother of Corn is discovered in the *milpa*, incense is burnt and ancient Mayan stories are remembered:

> Mother of Corn is the daughter of Lightning. Long long ago a man found a snake which had been hurt. The snake asked him to please take her home and he did. She lived with her father in a cave full of snakes. Her father was so grateful that he offered the man whatever he wanted as a reward for saving his daughter. About this time, the snakes turned into women and the man was dazzled by their looks. "No, I don't need anything," he said politely.
>
> "Do you have a wife?" asked Lightning. "I could give you one of my daughters."
>
> "That would be good," said the man, and he picked out the prettiest one, who just happened to be the snake he had saved out on the path. He took her for his wife. She was the Mother of Corn and if she harvested just one ear of corn from each corner of the field, it would multiply and her net would be filled with corn. She and her husband would have big fights because he thought she was picking all his corn. But she was just magic. One time when her husband hit her, Mother of Corn wiped the blood from her nose with an ear of corn. This is how the red corn came to be. Where Mother of Corn peed, the first squash vines grew, when she peed again, a *chayote* came up.
> —María Xila

At harvest time, ceremonies are held in the *milpa* to call the soul of the corn that didn't grow, or that was eaten by a raccoon.

> Soul of corn:
> come back from where the raccoon took you,
> from where the grackle ate you,

from the mole's tunnel,
the weevil's mouth,
the gopher hole,
the rat's den.
   —*Xpetra Ernándes Lópes*

Mother of the Fire is one of the three hearthstones in the center of the Mayan house.

Sacred fire:
Give me something to eat.
My griddle rests here,
Sacred stone.
I make my tortillas
on the face of your hearth.
On your mask of stone
I bake my bread.
   —*María Tzu*

 "The Three Hearthstones" or *Ox Yoket* is the name for the holiest mountain of the Zinacantecs. The Tzotzils consider the mountain tops to be sacred, especially if they are very high and have natural springs or caves at the summit. When such natural formations are lacking as a backdrop for rituals, cement altars and concrete grottos may be constructed as a stage for cosmic theater. All mountains are addressed as Fathermothers, the tutelary gods.

 The Earthquake Mother is one of four enormous snakes that hold the world on the tips of their tails. The Earth shakes when the snakes roll over.

Earthquake Mother:
Don't touch me.
Don't knock down my house
   —*Munda Tostón*

In downtown San Cristóbal, carved on the outside corner of the colonial palace of the conquistador Diego de Mazariegos, you can see the stone bas-relief of a mermaid with a serpent's tail whom the Chamulas call the Earthquake Mother.

Mother of Night can't sleep because the little red worms that live in her vagina keep her awake, and the only way to cure the itch is by making love with twelve or fifteen men. In his *Great Tzotzil Dictionary of San Lorenzo Zinacantán*, Robert M. Laughlin writes that loose women—and this includes those who laugh out loud—are punished in hell by having a red-hot wire stuck into their vaginas; but according to kitchen gossip, all women have little desire worms and want their husbands to do a good job in bed. Even though a man may hoe many rows of corn in a day, his wife expects him to make love to her twelve times each night to wear out those worms. They say there was a woman who was so promiscuous her animal spirit must have been a worm!

Mother of Ice can find treasure with a special mirror she has that also makes everything freeze over. After midnight if you see a shooting star that looks like a blue rattlesnake, you can be certain it is the Mother of Treasure. Where the star falls to Earth, you will find a machine for making money. As you dig, it helps to pray:

> Holy Snake:
> Please give me some pay.
> I want food
> and money.
> —*Munda Tostón*

Finding treasure will make you poorer than ever, because treasure, *takin*, is literally the "Sun's shit"; filthy money will always jinx you.

Mother Wind knocks down the cornfield. She is a two-headed woman—hair all tangled up with leaves and twigs—who walks very fast and is covered with bruises from bumping into trees and rocks that get in her way. She lives in a cave with the Lord of the Earth, and goes out in the sleet to steal the soul of the corn.

Wind has a scarlet heart,
she knocks down our *milpa*.
Wind is an envious thief
who steals our corn on the cob.
                —*Petú Bak Bolom*

The rainbow is called Mother of Evil, because she seals off the caves with her tail so the rain clouds can't get out. The colors of the rainbow come from her urine; cover yourself with your shawl when you look at her, or you'll get a headache. Spit tobacco juice at the rainbow, throw rocks at her, or three heads of garlic to frighten her away. Show her your penis or your pussy, but never point at a rainbow or your belly button will rot.

The rainbow bites me, *Kajval*.
She's spying on me,
chasing me into the house.
Get her out of here!
Run her off, *Kajval*!
                —*María Tzu*

For the ancient Maya, the "Great (or Red) Rainbow" *Chak-Chel* was the old Moon Goddess, the midwife of creation. Karen Bassie believes that *Chak-Chel* is from the Underworld because in classic iconography she is "pictured just as an Underworld deity with death eyes and death bones." The contemporary Txotzil rainbow is said to emerge from caves and to be evil. She is one of the *Pukuj*, a name that recalls *Ah Puch*, the god of death of the ancients. *Pukuj* are strong animal companions who suck the life out of other animal companions. They are evil *wayhel* who cause sickness.

There are *Pukuj* who steal babies out of the bellies of their mothers, or change them into monkeys. Some damage the Moon and the Sun. Daylight Savings Time is called *Pukuj* Time because it is said that the *Pukuj* have stolen an hour of light.

The Charcoal Cruncher's head comes off at night. She leaves her body in bed with her husband while her head bounces over to the fire so she can eat charcoal. As soon as the man realizes what is happening, he must put salt on the stump of her neck so the head won't stick on again when she come back to bed. Another *Pukuj, Yalem Bek'et,* the "Body Stripper," gets up at night and goes out to walk in the graveyard. She sits down next to a cross, pulls the flesh off her bones, then flies through the air as a skeleton.

The hummingbird that sings at night is a *Pukuj* errand boy for the Earth Lord who warns us of sickness or death. To soften a woman's heart, a man going courting takes along a hummingbird tied with green ribbon.

> Okay, Ámbar:
> If you don't want the *Pukuj*
> to come to your house in the night,
> bar the door,
> and rub garlic on your bedpost.
> —*Xalik Guzmán Bakbolom*

How can you tell in the dark if it's a real *Pukuj* who offers you his hummingbird? How can you tell the difference between your woman and the chimerical *Xpakinté* in a world where hummingbirds turn into bats?

HERE IN THE ABODE of the Tzotzils, the limestone mountain landscape is pockmarked with caves, sinkholes, grottos swallowing whole rivers, and springs where the water flows out of the rock. The cave is the setting for the mythical drama in which the Maya soul is a principal actor. In the Netherworld, death is transformed into life. Animal spirit companions and plumed serpents of ancient songs live within the Earth alongside the capricious Mayan gods and goddesses.

The Earth Goddess is *Kaxail* or *Kaxil,* a name that recalls the Yucatec Mayan word *kax* or *k'ax* meaning the uncultivated Earth. *Kaxail* is the Holy Wildwood, the Sacred Coffer Where the Secrets Are Kept. She is the supreme force of life, creator and mother of the Sun, the Moon, and all living beings, and she rules the forest primeval where life regenerates itself. The incantations for curing the soul are directed to her. Half the texts in this collection are for *Kaxail.*

I step and walk
on your flowering face,

Holy Mother,
Sacred Earth,

Mother Breast,
Holy Wildwood.

Show me the way, Mother,
put me on the right track.
          —Maruch Méndes Péres

The Earth is so great she cannot be seen, so powerful her true name is seldom mentioned directly. Instead, she is called *Our Mother on Whom We Tread*, the *Woman Who Appears in Dreams*, or *Me'me' Chuchu'*, "Mother Breast." Those who address her beg her pardon for having urinated and defecated on her face. Out of fear or reprisals from the Earth, animals hunted in the wild are referred to by euphemisms such *as te'tikal chij*—"wood sheep"—for a deer, or *ch'enal k'otz*—"cave chicken"—for quail. That which springs from her can be dangerous because of the great power she holds. One must ask her permission to plant the Earth with her son, her corn.

I'm going to dig a hole in your face, Sacred Earth.
I'm digging into your body.

I am planting my cornfield.
I am planting my work.

Fill my gourd, Holy Earth.
I want you to fill my bean pot.
          —Jwana te la Krus

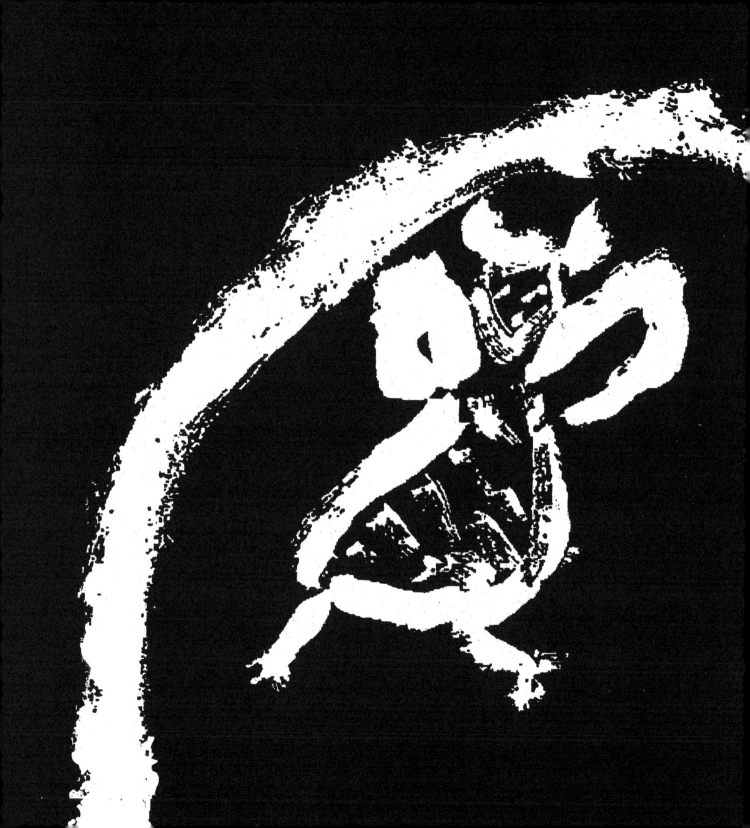

In *Perils of the Soul*, anthropologist Calixta Guiteras Holmes records the cosmic vision of Manuel Arias Sojom, a Tzotzil leader in San Pedro Chenalhó during the 1950s:

The Earth is the mother of universal life. She is the most compelling power in the universe. She is the supreme power. All others seem to form part of her or to have proceeded from her depths. She is goddess of the wilderness and mistress of the forest. Her wrath is easily roused and she bestows her gifts only when she is pleased.

She brings forth and fosters all creatures, but is simultaneously their common grave. She relentlessly swallows back, as a monster, the beings that she produces. All that live on her surface come from her interior and return there. She is all-producing, all maintaining, all-devouring.

The cosmic forces—fire, wind, rain, the eclipse, the earthquake—are manipulated by the earth. Disease and famine are manifestations of her wrathful moods. The forces of evil can be traced to the earth. Evil and good in man are related to his *wayhel*, the animal soul that makes him one with the earth.

She grudgingly tolerates man's living on her surface, and allows him to prey on her creatures. She takes advantage of any opportunity to drag man's *ch'ulel* into her recesses. When she is offended by the stench of human excrement, she will sicken man and prevent his recovery. She resents procreation.

Her deadly creatures of darkness are related to the destructive sky gods. Her instruments of evil are the *Pukuj* and the *Potzlom*.

Direct contact with all that is brought in from her wilderness and to man's use is deadly, and destroys fertility. Things from the wild can only be tamed by those who possess the esoteric knowledge.

It is *Kaxail*, the Earth, who is first invoked in prayer. It is in her power to exchange an evil *wayhel* for a good one. She is asked for life, for health, for protection. She is asked to kill and to destroy.

She is the cause of all harm that may befall the entire group. Only by obtaining her permission may man occupy her with his home and his fields. Any change of residence, any enlargement of the *milpa*, must be her gift.

She punishes and destroys. She commands continual respect and sacrifice. Her protection can be acquired only with constant care and vigilance and is forfeited by the slightest breach or misdemeanor. She is man's conscience and appears to him in the guise of a woman; her commands are strictly obeyed.*

Potters ask permission of the Earth before making use of her clay. Maruch Méndes Péres worked as a child in the house of a potter; the old woman sang as she kneaded her clay:

> Holy Earth: I need you,
> I work you.
> You will sustain me,
> you will buy me food and drink.
> —*Beronika Uch*

The Tzotzils invoke the Earth before using her mud for plastering their houses; they beg her leave before cutting trees for house beams, firewood or for making charcoal:

> Don't kill me, don't fall on me,
> Sacred Tree, Sacred Pine.
> It's because I am in need
> that I cut down
> your Sacred Tree, your Sacred Vine,
> Holy Earth, Holy Sky.
> —*Antonia Moshán Culej*

The Earth has a dark side that draws beings into her dangerous depths: she is the mother in a rage who whips her children, the *Pukuj* who wears a mask with the face of the sweetheart, concealing her wild matted hair. She opens her jaws during an earthquake, blows down the *milpa* with her breath, kidnaps souls and animal companions, devouring those who dare live in a mud house without asking for permission with animal sacrifice and a gift of song. To inaugurate a house constructed on the face of the Earth with her mud and thatch, an old woman is called upon to light the first fire in the hearth and placate the Earth with prayers:

> We are going to sleep here.
> We are going to rest here.
>
> We are going to sin here.
> We are going to make love.
>
> Protect us from being bitten
> by a vine or a stick.
>
> Save us from being devoured
> by your new thatch, the shiny nails
>
> We offer you gifts, *Kaxail*,
> so the new house won't eat the people in it.
> —*Xunka' Utz'utz' Ni'*

Mesoamerican archeologist Karl Taube associates the Mayan Earth goddess with the Aztec "Earth Lord" *Tlatecuhtli*, which he calls "a monstrous devouring being clearly depicted as female." The ancient Mayans related the Earth to the Young Maize God, whom Tzotzil shaman Maruch Méndes Péres calls the Son of *Kaxail*. As this book goes to press, Maruch showed Carter Wilson and me a dozen stalactites she keeps on her altar in between two wooden crosses adorned with pine boughs. Maruch called our attention to the resemblance between the stalactites and ears of corn. She insists they are the "saints" of *Kaxail* and must be treated with great reverence. To illustrate her point, she tells a story about stalactites:

> When I was a child, a neighbor found many stalactites in a cave. A boy helped the man carry them home and they threw them in a pile in the yard. Little girls

played with them as though they were dolls, they dressed them and carried them in their shawls. Children played with the stalactites and little by little the stones became lost among the weeds.

One day during Carnival, the five Lost Days, the neighbor was cooking up a great pot of *atole* outside his house. The *maxes*, who dress as monkeys, were dancing around and singing when a huge snake appeared out of nowhere. It was as thick as a man's leg, very long and it glittered just like the crystals inside stalactites. No one had ever seen a snake like this: it glowed blue-green and it climbed up onto the roof of the house. All the people who were gathered around for the fiesta saw it.

The snake slithered into the house through the thatch and was crawling along the rafters inside. The seers were summoned, and they spit liquor at it, they threw handfuls of snuff at the snake to make it dizzy.

The serpent crawled down to the floor and curled up in a spiral. The neighbor struck it on the head with a stick, he killed it and skinned it, throwing the meat to the vultures.

That night the seers dreamed the Earth was angry because of the stalactites. They gathered up the broken stones, they took the doll clothes off and returned them to the cave. The seers dreamed again and the Earth told them she didn't want the stalactites back, they had been defiled and she didn't want them anymore. What she wanted was human lives.

The neighbor who had found the stalactites came down with a fever that killed him in three days. The boy who had helped him carry the stalactites and one of the girls who had played with them also became sick, but the seers burned incense in the cave and prayed, and the children survived.

Once when I was watching my sheep down by the river, I slipped and fell down the embankment in a landslide of rocks and earth. One of the sheep broke her leg, a little lamb was killed. I dreamed that night that a foreign woman led the lamb away tied to a cord. I understood this to be the Lord of the Earth and I realized she had also led my soul away. Now my soul was working as her maid. My soul swept the Earth Lord's house, washed her clothes, cared for her children.

I realized that my soul actually LIKED working for the Earth Lord, she was getting used to eating chicken every day. At least my soul thought it was chicken, I knew it was snakes she was fattening me up on.

I became very angry with my soul. I paid the seer to pray for her to come back, and she did, but she'd only stay with me for a couple of days before she ran off to the Earth Lord again.

This was very upsetting. My soul didn't want to be with me anymore and I just couldn't put up with this situation any longer. I cut three switches and began to hit the Earth. I yelled at the Earth. I gave her a good scolding.

'Give me my soul back!' I shouted. I didn't drink any liquor or burn candles or sacrifice a black hen. No. I just beat the Earth and yelled:

> 'Earth: I don't owe you a thing.
> I have not sinned.
> I'm just dizzy, I'm just stupid.
> I fell down, I slipped.
> Don't tie me up!
> I never wanted your gold!
> I never asked you for corn!
> I don't want your beans!
> I never asked for anything.
> You have no reason to make me your slave,
> I won't be your servant,
> Sacred Mother, Holy *Kaxail*,
> Holy Earth, Sacred Sky,
> Sacred Soil, Holy Land.
> Holy King, Sacred *Ajau*,
> Holy Snake, Sacred *Chauk*.'
> —*Maruch Méndes Péres*

Chauk is another name for Earth Lord, *Yajval Banumil,* often described as a fat rich *kaxlan,* "foreigner," who lives in caves and controls natural resources including rain and buried treasure. In prayers, he is often addressed as King.

Is *Chauk* the consort of the Earth? If so, this mixed race marriage mirrors the Conquest and the subsequent domination of *Kaxail* by alien gods and men who possess the Earth, taking her when they will. María Gutiérrez is of the opinion, however, that *Chauk* is the offspring of the Earth, "a child born of rape who came to no good." The Earth Lord is a *Pukuj* bastard son gone bad who has taken over the running of estates and the administration of rents. It seems there are many Earth Lords now, many *Kaxlanes.* The old Earth lives in hiding, her powers scourged by Inquisition, torture, and self-racism. In Renaissance Europe, witches, infidels and devils were hunted and burned. The culture of the New World was damned and condemned to death in the name of God.

The European invasion of the land of the Earth Mother in the sixteenth-century drove the Mayan goddesses underground in fear and humiliation, displaced by imported gods of great splendor and power. The Earth is violated; she gives birth to half-castes who suppress the language, culture, and religion of their mother. The Lords are ashamed of her and wear the mask of their father's gods, repudiating the Earth as primitive, pagan, a stepdaughter to filth and witchcraft. The new Christians were taught to fear nature and to consider the woods to be savage and dangerous, a place for shitting and throwing garbage. The vanquished are forced to live in towns, they grow ashamed of thatch and mud, as though the Earth were a sickness they do not want to catch.

When a goddess falls from favor she is bound to be accused of evil. Just about the only surviving female descendant of the Earth Mother is the malignant *Xpakinté,* the Woman of the Woods, who tricks drunks on their way home at night. At first she appears to be the poor fellow's own wife, but then she lures him down the wrong path to his death, over a cliff, impaled on a maguey cactus. The Fathermothers of Yucatán called her *Ix Paclah Actun,* "She Who Fornicates in Caves." If embraced, the *Xpakinté* becomes a rotten tree trunk. Her head is found to be hollow in the back, filled with furry caterpillars that sting like fire. A man must take off his pants to save himself from her—and then put them on again inside out.

Even though the Earth Goddess is now considered old-fashioned and never mentioned among the men, contemporary Tzotzil women continue directing most of their incantations to her. To ask for rain to make her *milpa* grow, Maruch Méndes Péres addresses *Kaxail*, the Earth, and then *Chauk*, the Earth Lord:

> Sacred Mother, Sacred Breast,
> Sacred *Kaxail*,
> Holy Earth, Holy Ground,
> Holy Thunderbolt,
> Sacred *Ahau*,
> Holy Snake,
> Holy *Chauk*:
> Fill my mouth with food.

Prayers are said in caves, springs, and forest shrines:

> Father Thunder,
> Mother Thunder:
> We don't want lightning.
> Nor roaring thunder, nor hail.
> Just water, *Kajval*,
> to wet the dust,
> to end this drought that bites us.
> —*María Xila*

Father Thunder, Mother Thunder refer to *Chauk*, great-grandson of the ancient Maya rain god *Chac*, who sends the rain and the lightning bolts. Each year, in the dry season, *Chauk* travels to Guatemala on the back of a deer to bring back gunpowder for his lightning bolts. His whip is a snake and his saddle an armadillo. *Chauk's* daughters, the *Anjel*, are maidens who take on the form of snakes. They fluff up the clouds inside the caverns, preparing them as they would cotton for spinning.

It is rumored that the Earth Lord's caves run from Guatemala City to the Highlands of Chiapas. A little past the Tzeltal Maya town of Tenejapa, a whole river suddenly disappears inside an immense grotto at Yochi'b, which has been a market place since before Columbus. A few years ago, after several days of underground exploration, a group of Italians wearing black wet suits and accompanied by a huge white dog came out of the cave. The frightened market crowd took them for the living dead who had gotten lost in the bowels of the Earth. The spelunkers had to run for their lives.

Another traveler in the Underworld, linguist and epigrapher Barbara McLeod, discovered a one-thousand-year-old Mayan altar at the end of a fifteen-day walk within the Earth beneath Belize. One time she and archaeologist Dennis Puleston lost their way inside another cave. They were just about to starve to death when, hallucinating collectively, they saw a shining creature with a body like a glyph who led them to the exit.

Later, in the Mayan ruins of Chichén Itza, Dennis Puleston discovered an underground chamber with stalactites stuck onto the ceiling, forming a kind of infraworld xylophone. After invoking *Chac* by striking music from the stalactites, the archaeologist climbed the steps of the Castle of Quetzalcoatl where, out of a clear blue sky, he was struck dead by a lightning bolt.

THERE'S AN OLD STORY about a girl from Tenejapa who married Lightning and created a lake. Her name was Suyul and she was just a babe in arms. Her mother had carried her out by the spring and was trying to wash clothes. Suyul was crying and crying. She wouldn't calm down until her mother put her into a puddle of water.

Suyul slapped the water with her hands, she struck the water as a baby does, saying:

Ti suyul ti suyul ti suyul.

Suyul was playing in the water, digging in the mud, and in just a little while she made a big lake. "Go away; I'm staying here," the baby told her mother. "Because I am not yours anymore. I'm going to where the Lightning lives."

Now it was the mother who cried and cried; "*Ay Kajval!*" the mother said. She didn't want to go home without her little baby. She didn't want to leave her there all alone.

"OK," said Baby Suyul, "in thirteen days you can come back. But bring me my skirts and my necklaces. Get everyone together playing harp, playing pretty guitar, lighting firecrackers. Burn rows of candles, I want lots of candles," ordered Suyul.

In thirteen days they brought drums, they brought trumpets, they brought music. And when they got to where the puddle had been before, Suyul was swimming in a huge lake. She was a grownup woman. Suyul asked for embroidered blouses, she asked for skirts, she asked for everything.

> The cloths are carried,
> the clothes are washed.
>
> They are taking them to the Virgin,
> giving them to the lake.
>
> They put the weavings in a gourd;
> they throw it, spinning it around
>
> and around,
> down
>
> to the Lady of the Lake,
> to her spring
>
> where the water
> is born.
>   *—María Xila*

THE SUN HAS THIRTEEN SHIRTS in thirteen colors for the thirteen steps of the sky. He puts on the white shirt when he shines, the green shirt when it rains, his red shirt when it thunders. At night he wears all thirteen.

Known as *The Scribe*, the Sun carries a book in which he writes down everything that happens each day. You can tell when he is writing because a halo appears around him. At night he goes into his sweatbath beneath the Earth.

Each dawn a Chamula girl—the planet Venus—sweeps the path in the sky, preceding the Sun in his way across the heavens. Behind Our Sun walks his mother, the Holy Moon.

The Sun asked his mother for a shirt. She picked some cotton and beat it with a dogwood stick so it would mat like felt. She cut a hole for the neck with her machete. The Sun put on his new shirt and went for a walk in the woods. The cotton was pulled apart by the thorns and the first shirt of the Sun disappeared in the bushes. The cotton became the fog of the cloud forest, high up on the mountain tops where we go to pray.
—*Petú Xantis*

At the beginning of time, Mother Moon taught the Fathermothers to spin and weave. She climbed up a *ceiba*, the sacred Mayan silk-cotton tree, and she formed her loom with the branches; she carved her spindle from the twigs. With the cotton silk of the tree, she spun the first thread and wove the first *huipil*. This done, she climbed the notches of her warping stick into the sky to become the Moon Goddess.

Long ago women made threads as today we make our children:
They spun them with the strength of their bodies.

When the Earth began, they say, the Moon climbed a tree.
There she was weaving, there she was spinning in the tree.

"Learn to weave," she said to the First Fathermothers.
"Learn to spin!" That's how weaving began.
—*Loxa Jiménes Lópes*

HANDS WEAVE THE WOOL, but it is the soul of the loom that creates the *huipil*. Through poetry, the artisan tames her weaving sticks and charms her spindles, engaging their spirit so work can be done. Unless tools are well treated, they may rebel. The sacred book of the ancient Maya, the *Popol Vuh*, tells of an insurrection of the cooking pots who attacked their heartless masters saying,

You hurt us,
burning our mouths,
charring our faces on the fire.
You burnt us even though
we did no wrong.
When it's your turn,
you too will burn.

In order for them to do their job, tools must be sung to and fed. Spindles are kept in a basket of corn and the spun thread is given *ul*, corn gruel, to eat before the weaver measures out the warp of her loom. Otherwise, the cloth might shrink from hunger.

One must also feed musical instruments and give them moonshine *pox* to drink, spraying a mouthful onto the strings of the harp while praying:

Sacred Music,
Holy Harp:
Here's a little nip
to lighten your heart.
   —Xpetra Ernándes

It is said that a work reflects the state of the soul of the artisan who performed it. If a weaver is sad, her loom will become tangled. If she dies before her weaving is finished, her soul will never find rest. If a farmer is not joyful, her corn will not sprout and the soul of the corn will suffer within the Earth. To keep the gods and the saints happy, they must be fed on incense and endless songs.

THE FAITH OF THE MODERN MAYA is syncretic, woven from the animistic religion of the First Fathermothers, Renaissance Catholicism, and postmodern Protestant fundamentalism. Christ is the Sun and the Virgin Mary the Moon.

You have seen my Ten Holy Heavens,
the Ten Blues of the Sky,

Mother Moon, you have watched me,
you have seen

that I am not stealing,
Mother Moon, Holy Virgin, Kajval.
    —Mikaela Moshán Culej

Kajval—from the ancient Maya *Ahau*—means Our Lords and Protectors: the Earth, the Moon, the Sun, *Cristo*, the Virgins, the saints. The adversaries of the *Kajval* are known as *Pukuj*.

When envious *Pukuj* try to steal the light from the sky during an eclipse, women pray and cry out to scare them off, beating on their griddles and pots to protect the Sun and the Moon from death. During a lunar eclipse, women leave a gourd filled with water in the yard so that the Moon might wash her face. It is said that when the Moon turns as red as blood, many women die. Antonia Moshán Culej, Roselia Montoya, and Xpetra Ernándes watched as the face of the full Moon turned dark during the eclipse in 1996, and cried with great sadness because they did not know whether the Mother Moon would survive her bout with the *Pukuj*. During a solar eclipse, María Tzu prays so the *Potzlom* won't eat the Sun:

> We can't tell if dawn will come back
> to the sky, *Kajval.*
>
> Something is devouring,
> Something is destroying, *Kajval.*

Way up in the sky, higher than the thirteen steps of heaven, there is a floating platform loaded with lighted candles, one for each person who had ever lived in the world. When a candle goes out, someone dies. Witches can shorten lives by shaving wax off the candles. Bargains can be struck with the Bearer of Time to make one's life longer.

Elder Brother Who Feeds the Souls:
Guardian of the Corral:
Bearer of Time:

Keep my animal alive
for many years

with pine pitch,
with tree sap,

with rose water,
with fir cone,

laurel knot,
and thirteen essences of *tilil*.

Make my days longer
with the sweat of your legs,

with your hands
that glow green

as precious jade,
your green, green blood.
                    —*Manwela Kokoroch*

MAYAN WOMEN HAVE POWERS to extend their lives, and to protect themselves from evil. One form of benevolent magic for taming higher forces, called *Yaluat*, consists of taking one's clothes off, baring the naked soul before an adversary. A Chamula woman may tame a wild sheep by raising her skirts and putting the animal's muzzle in her private parts. In Zinacantán

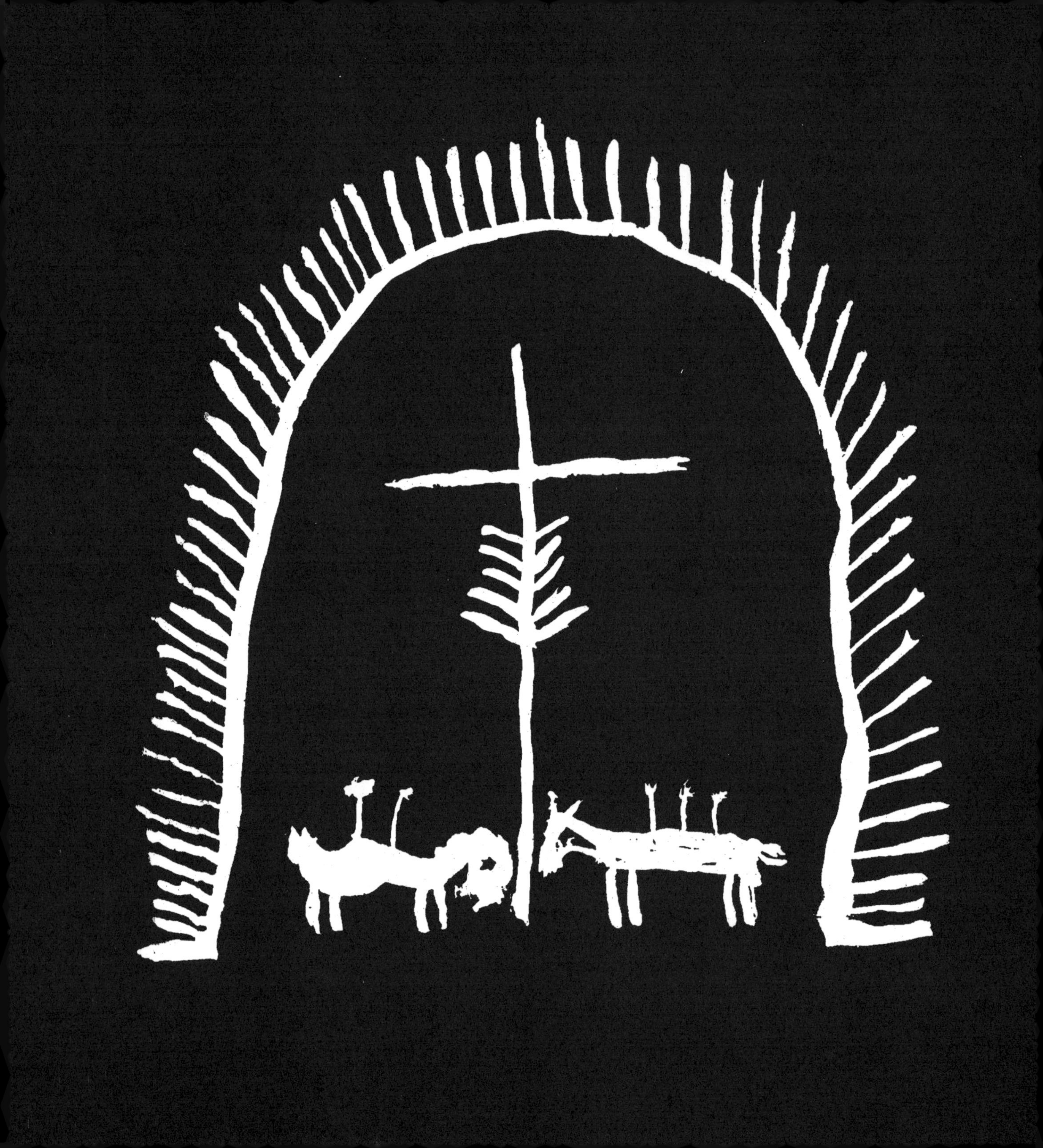

during the Christmas dances that represent bullfights, women lift up their skirts to distract the bull. The *Popol Vuh* tells how, to defend his domain against invaders, the king of the K'iche sent his daughters to bathe in the river in view of the enemy army, instructing them to detain the soldiers with nude charms. Similarly, a day before the conquest of Chamula in 1524, young women of Zinacantán were sent to the waterhole to bathe in an attempt to stop the advance of the invading Spanish troops. This place, where today women wash clothes, is known as *Tz'ajom Pik*, "Submerged Clitoris."

A priestess or goddess, surrounded by clay idols within a cloud of incense, was carried by the Chiapaneco Indian soldiers during the battle they sustained with the Spanish earlier in the 1524 campaign, here described by conquistador Bernal Díaz del Castillo:

> The woman on the litter and the young girls who escorted her were nude, their bodies painted and adorned with brightly colored macaw feathers and bolls of white cotton.

Wouldn't you like to imagine Spanish soldiers overtaken by this splendor throwing down their harquebusses to join in the pagan rites? The chronicles, however, report a massacre. Cathedrals were built using stones from the pyramids. The goddesses went into hiding, but their words have never ceased to inspire the Mayans to defend themselves against their oppressors.

The Maya rebellions of 1712 and 1869 in Chiapas were led by women who incited the men to take up arms. Agustina Kómes Checheb was directed by clay idols and accompanied by a saint called the Mother of War. Many women fought alongside their husbands in hope that the coldness attributed to females might cool down the enemy's artillery fire. Chamulas who took part in the Indian movement of 1911 tell how forty-five virgins from their town ambushed the Federal Army. They lifted up their skirts and threatened the soldiers with their sex, brandishing weaving sticks and yelling: "We advance with red *huipils*! Onward with red *huipils*!"

During the Mexican Revolution, the troops of Obregón and Pineda hid in a cave on the sacred mountain of Mother Chaklajún. The mouth of the cave closed in on them and the soldiers were trapped inside. According to Xalik Guzmán Bakbolom, they are still there; when the sky thunders you can hear them firing their cannon. Xunka' Utz'utz' Ni' begs Mother Chaklajún to defend her people from the armies that have threatened for hundreds of years. Her prayer *So the*

Armies Won't Come is from January of 1994 when the National Army sexually assaulted Mayan women all over Chiapas:

> Don't let them torture us.
> Don't let them rape us
> in our houses, in our homes.

Violence is enough to drive you crazy. María Kartones covers her face with mud and screams, *"Protect me from the soldiers. They are killing me AAAAAAY!"* reflecting the horrors of war that scar women's lives forever and drive them from their homes.

THE VIRGIN was trying to find a place to live. Who knows how many years she searched? Who knows where she started out from? Maybe she came out of a cave or down from the sky, no one knows. They say only that she came to this land with her brothers and sisters. Saint Juan Chamula was the elder brother and Saint Marta the littlest girl. They walked over from the other side of the sea carrying their little siblings in their shawls: Saint Pegro, Saint Pablo, and Saint Antrés. They were looking for a place to live. They went through Jitotol, they went through Plátanos, through Chabajebal, "The Place of the Cornfields," but couldn't live in these places. There were too many mosquitoes, the land was too hot.

The Virgin was trying to find a place to build her house. No one knows how long she had been looking. When she arrived here she climbed a tree with great branches so she could see way off into the distance. There she was, way up in the tree, covered with resin and beeswax. The Virgin saw this was a good place to stay. Her daughters could live here.

"I want my house," she said, and the men and women came together to build the town because the Virgin wanted it so. The men built the church and the women the courthouse, the House of the Women. They made the mortar of mud with lime and egg yolk. They called to the stones and beams:

> "Rise up vine, rise up tree, rise up vine, rise up tree," they said, and with a tre-
> mendous sound the timber came to them—all by itself—no one had to carry it on a
> tumpline.

We can't get the beams to come to us now, nor the stones. We are not as strong as we used to be. We don't know the words anymore. We can't say the spells.

—*María Álvares Jiménes, Me' Avrila*

Nevertheless, the saints continue to speak to Mayan women. The Virgin calls to Loxa Jiménes Lópes in dreams, inviting her to take the *cargo* of *Martoma Sakramento*:

Please, carry me.
Please, with harps and rattles!

The tradition of the *cargo* system is one of community service: noble, sacred work, a sacrifice of time and money for the saints, the gods and goddesses. During a time, usually a year, the *cargo*holder carries the weight of the universe for her community. The *Martomas* who keep the saints burn incense before the images and carry them on their pilgrimages. They must learn to recite many hours of ritual couplets as part of the fiesta. The stage for this extravaganza, once the pyramid and ball court, is now the town square and the street. Those who produce the sacred dramas and play the main roles can earn great prestige in the eyes of the community. They also go into debt for the rest of their lives paying for the music, fireworks, candles, flowers, incense, liquor, tamales, and even bulls for sacrifice. In this way the wealth of a few is, ideally, shared with everyone in the community.

Apart from the *cargos* for a man and his wife together, there are one or two for single women. In Tenejapa, the Moon's Weavers are women who devotedly create the clothes for the Virgin. In Chenalhó, the *Me' Tzebetik*, the "Mother of the Girls," dedicates her life to teaching rites and spells to young women. In Chamula, prestigious widows or virgins are chosen to attend the birth of the *Ch'ul Niño*, the Christ Child, the new Son who is also the new Sun. They dance and lull him with their songs. María Patixtán Likán Chitom has this *cargo* now; she is known as *Martoma Sakramento*. Her whole house has been turned into an altar, pine needles are spread on the floor, various kinds of bromeliad flowers adorn the enormous crosses outside and in. The *cargo*holder's house is filled with incense, the splendor of the shining candles and the song of the harp. The *Martoma* undresses in front of all those gathered in her house, she takes a ritual bath, then puts on her ceremonial black *huipil* adorned with yarn and ribbons, plaiting pompons of colors into her braids. The midwives to the *Ch'ul Niño* spend Christmas Eve singing to the child who has come into the world:

> I am a girl, my girl.
> I am a woman, my woman.
>
> I am your reflection in the mirror.
> I am just like you.
>
> I am woman, I am women.
> I am girl, I am girls.
>
> Woman, Mother of the Sky.
> I am a girl, Mother of Happiness.
>
> I am the *Martoma.*
> I am the girl *Martoma* of San Juan.
>
> You are a woman, a woman
> You are a girl, a girl.
> —*María Patixtán Likán Chitom*

A NEWBORN BABY GIRL is presented with the implements of a woman's work: the spindle, the carding combs, the weaving sticks, the grinding stone, a tumpline for carrying firewood.

> Here is a tumpline
> to help you with your burden
> when you gather kindling
> for the fire
> to keep you warm,

to cook your food,
to boil the water.
                    —*Rosa Xulemhó*

The midwife puts a pinch of salt in the baby's mouth, a taste of chile, saying:

When you grow up,
when you can speak,

you will work in the cornfield,
you will weave,

you will earn money
to buy your salt.
                    —*Rosa Xulemhó*

Little by little the child learns her mother's work. A wife is known as the Owner of the House or the Mistress of the Bed. Often she is already married when she begins to menstruate. The young man comes courting, bringing cane liquor, bread, meat, cigarettes, and of course, money, to ask for her hand. At the suitor's first visit, the parents of the girl contend they have no children, no children at all. The second time the young man comes calling they might admit to having a daughter, but say she is very lazy. "The only thing she knows how to do is to eat candied pumpkin," they tell the boy.

Xalik Guzmán Bakbolom became annoyed when he read Xpetra Ernándes's prayer titled *So the Dog Won't Bark at My Boyfriend*. Xalik insisted, "Even though Xpetra says the fiancée talks to the dog, this is not true. The girl isn't even supposed to know anyone has come to ask for her hand." The young couple never speak to one another during courtship. "Well, that is how it was before," Xalik admits. "Now the girls have gone crazy. They go out looking for the boys and give themselves freely without asking any bride price. In the old days wives were asked for and paid for."

Xpetra laughs at Xalik's allegations. "What does he know?" she says. "The fathers have no idea the boyfriend comes courting secretly, because the dog doesn't bark. The girl prays so he can sneak over without her father finding out about it. It's true a girl shouldn't talk to boys, but with one look you can say everything." Love charms are important for getting your man:

> I want him to talk to my body.
> I want his blood to ache for me
> when he sees me on the way to the market.
> I want to join myself to him.
> I want this man to be my other half.
>   —*Xpetra Ernándes*

In *The Great Tzotzil Dictionary of San Lorenzo Zinacantán*, Robert M. Laughlin mentions that when the parents of a girl don't accept the proposal of marriage, the boy's family throws water on the fire and the ashes fly through the air.

Calixta Guiteras Holmes writes that in Cancuc in the 1940s men could buy a permit from the town mayor to enable them to kidnap any woman they liked. A widow with no desire to remarry would have to pay a fee to the civil authorities so she wouldn't be abducted. The great majority of Mayan women confess they were married off or, as they say, sold by their fathers to men they had never seen before. Their first sexual experience—known in Tzotzil as the bite of the bat—is in effect rape. However, as time goes by some women come to care for their husbands. As in other cultures, the ritual phrases you hear at weddings express an ideal that often differs from the reality of everyday life. Many women of the new generation are simply not getting married; they work, earn their own money, and support their children alone, asking, "Why put up with a drunk who beats me?"

Domestic violence due to alcoholism is the universal theme of the Tzotzil lullabies.

> Go to sleep little baby, go to sleep.
> Your daddy's drunk
>
> and if he hits me,
> I'm running to the woods.
>   —*Petra Tzon Te' Vitz*

A newborn baby boy is presented with a tiny pine torch, according to Romín Teratol of Zinacantán, so in the dark of night he can guide his drunken dad home.

Still it is considered important that a man be present at birth to give the mother strength and support. She kneels on a palm straw mat, holding onto the back of a chair or a rope hung from the rafters, and prays to the Mother of the Most Difficult:

> Don't deliver me to darkness.
> Don't abandon me to the night.
> —*Munda Tostón*

When a baby cries, her mama will rub the baby's private parts to make her happy and pray to the Mother Breast, the *Me'me' Chuchu'*, so she herself will have milk. Clay drums are referred to as breasts in Chamula; they resemble cooking pots and may represent the abundance of the Mother Earth, who is also called "Sacred Breast." Stillborn babies are suckled by a breast tree in the Underworld. The mother who has lost her child prays that she might forget her pain:

> Little dead one, my gift,
> my suffering, my son,
>
> my ear of corn
> just beginning to grow.
>
> Let him be gone from my memory,
> Flowering Mother of the Sky.
> —*Loxa Jiménes Lópes*

YOU HAVE TO BURY THE DEAD WELL, preferably under the floor of the house. Together with the corpse should go all the hair combings and fingernail clippings from her whole life, a ball of ground black maize, and a gourd for drinking *matz*. Women save their most beautiful *huipils* for their burial. If the dead woman has held a *cargo*, she is dressed in ceremonial clothes, ribbons and necklaces. Only at the wakes of the poorest is there no harp. It is better to do without a coffin than to have a funeral with no singing.

A candle is put into the hands of a dead woman and called her "companía" so she will not feel alone and call another living person to accompany her into the Underworld. A few coins are tucked in with her to buy sugar beer or sweet lemons on the way to *K'atinbak*, the "Place Where the Bones Are Warmed."

We have to cross a lake to get there. A river of blood. A black dog carries us on his back. That is why we talk gently to the black dog. You mustn't hit him nor kill him, but give him a tortilla every day and pray to him so he will take us to where we have to go. My parents call to me. They are dead now. "Come, daughter," they say. "Come with us," they say. I don't want to go. I am so used to not being dead.
    —Me' Avrila

When you give the dog his food, you pray to him so he will help you when the time comes:

Good dog:
Take your tortilla.
When I die,
you will carry me
across the water
to *K'atinbak*.
    —Munda Tostón

The souls of the dead work for the Earth Lord and visit their families once a year on the Day of the Dead. When the dead are born again, the men will become women and the women men.

HERE IN THE BELLYBUTTON OF THE WORLD, as the Tzotzil call their homeland, the women live very much apart from the men. With the exception of married couples, women and men do not speak to each other, a contrast to the occidental tradition of not speaking after marriage. In Tzotzil, "to speak" implies "to have sex." When a woman must talk to a man who is not her husband, she will cover her mouth with her hand and avoid looking him in the face. Due to the distance between the sexes, women have maintained their own cosmologies the men know nothing about.

To see how separate the universes of men and women might really be, we enlisted the help of Xalik Guzmán Bakbolom, co-translator of the texts in this book, who knows just about everything a Tzotzil man can know about his culture. Xalik Guzmán Bakbolom started working as an informant for anthropologists from the University of Chicago and Harvard almost fifty years ago. Over a lifetime, he has transcribed thousands of hours of tape in which scores of Tzotzil men were interviewed about all aspects of life. Here is what this scholar said about the goddesses Tzotzil women address in their spells:

> Mother of Night, I don't know.
> Mother of the Month, not either,
> Mother of Wind, don't know.
> Mother of Hail, more or less.
> Mother of Corn, don't know.
> Mother Breast, don't know.
> Mother of Mist, don't know.
> Woman's Rock, don't know.
> Mother Earth, don't know.
> Mother of Water, don't know.
> Mother of the Hearth, don't know.
> Don't know anything about these things.
> My father is dead and he never
> mentioned any of this at all.

The separation of the sexes is also reflected in the division of labor into men's work and women's work. I've only heard of two Mayan men who could weave, for example, and they were looked upon as outcasts. One was from Zinacantán and he wore a skirt. He was said to be a witch and a trader; he and his wife would walk all the way down to hot country peddling their wares, both of them wearing skirts.

Tzotzil men make fun of a coward saying that he has a "blue ass," because skirts dyed with indigo tint women's buttocks navy blue. The women walk down the path behind the men, who may be riding horses. María Gutiérrez met such a pair on the road and asked the man: "Why is the woman walking when you ride?" She says he answered, "Because she has no horse." In rural taxis, the men occupy the seats; the women go in the trunk. In some villages, women are treated with more respect than in others. Women in Chamula can own land and the Zapatistas have introduced universal suffrage, which—although guaranteed by the Mexican constitution—had been a privilege for males only in the Highlands of Chiapas. In Zinacantán, a relatively prosperous community, women seem to have to ask a man's permission for just about everything.

> But in Venustiano Carranza, it's the woman who tells the man what to do. They go down to the river to wait for the mule drivers who pass by on their way to the mountains, and when a man comes near them they transform themselves into bulls, run after the men, and try to gore them with their horns. If the man flees, he'll turn into a woman and won't be able to leave there ever. How could he go home as a woman? How would he explain it to his wife?
> —*Guadalupe Domínguez*

Tales of men turning into women often spice up the gossip among the *comagres*:

> A long time ago a couple of compadres wanted to know which one had the biggest penis. They climbed up on a rock which was still soft to measure theirs, but found them changed into vaginas; the compadres were now women.
> —*Munda Tostón*

In Chamula there is said to be a stone called *Pisom At*, the "Penis Measurer," where males may compare themselves with giants. In Zinacantán there is talk of *Antzil Ton*, the "Woman's Rock," but nobody will say what it's for.

In Chenalhó there are several important lifetime *cargos* held by men who dress as women during Carnival, including the *Me'el* or "Mother," the *Me' Ka'benal* or "Lacandón Maya Mother," and the "Guatemalan Mother," representing a Central American prostitute who caters to soldiers. Among their many duties, the Mothers conduct well-attended sex education sessions as one of the rituals during "Crazy February," the five lost days of the Mayan calendar. These performances take place on straw mats in the houses of the religious officials and the young are encouraged to pay attention. The naughty Elder Brother *Ik'al* addresses the children in a playful tone, reciting bawdy couplets about coupling:

This is how we do it.
Each taking his turn.

Check out these positions
husbands and wives can learn.

Later that night other transvestites, the *Antzil Ak'ot*, "Dancing Women," sing on the church steps: "I am half woman, I am half girl."

In Carnival in Chamula, the *Senyora de Nana María Kokorina* is played by a man who personifies La Malinche—Cortes' Amerindian mistress and interpreter. There are also men who dress as the "Perfumed Woman," the *J-xinulán*, during the fiesta of San Sebastián in Zinacantán, impersonating and ridiculing "loose" foreign women who comb their hair in public and stink of toilet water.

I am a perfumed woman.
I am a perfumed girl.
I am a bought woman.
I am a paid girl.
I am a puta woman.
I am a puta girl.
The Sun is dancing.
The Moon is dancing.
          —*Tonik Nibak*

THE FATHERMOTHERS taught the Tzotzil incantations for every occasion. There are magic words to win the love of a man, and others to kill him if he is unfaithful. Verses to lull the baby and to cure the loco:

We will shake him thirteen times
so he stops counting
his heartbeats.

So the devils will stop teasing him.
So the *Pukuj* will leave off frying him.
— *Xunka' Utz'utz' Ni'*

The women sing to borrow a gourd from the neighbor or to order a water jug from the potter:

Find me the Earth,
find me the clay,

to make my pot,
to make my jar.
— *María Tzu*

Or to ask for help in preparing the fiesta:

Tire yourself to death
preparing my sweet beer.

Lend me your tiger
to carry my sugarcane.

Because there's not enough drink,
there's not enough strong *chicha*.
— *María Álvares Jiménes, Me' Avrila*

The seers burn *copal* and say spells so drunks will stop drinking and the Catholics will leave off fighting over teetotalism with the heavily-armed Protestants:

Let them have a drink,
Let it go down smooth.

Let them lose their heads,
so they don't remember their AK-47s.
　　　　　—Xunka' Utz'utz' Ni

Tzotzil women compose verses and more verses for the endless Drunken Women's Song.
They sing to the Sacred Virgin and to the Godmother of Drunk Women.

I am the drunken woman.
I am the drunken girl.

You gave me my drunkenness.
Godmother of the Drunks.

I feel very sweet.
I feel very sour.

This booze has a taste like a melon.
Like watermelon.

The vapor from the kettle,
the sweat of the coiling snake,
the rum that rinses out the barrel.
　　　　　—Maruch Méndes Péres

Maruch Méndes Péres sings to the coil of her clandestine still and also to the penis with its
head like a firemen's helmet or little hat, *sombrerito*:

Sombrerito today.
Sombrerito tomorrow.

I want *sombrerito*, *Kajval ooo*.
Give me *sombrerito*, *Sagrado Pagre*.

La la ti la la bi.
La la ti la la bi.

I drank, *Kajval*.
I am drunk, *Sagrado Pagre*.

Bolom Chon in the sky,
Bolom Chon on the Earth.

Bolom Chon, title of the most popular Tzotzil song, means jaguar, according to Xalik Guzmán Bokblom. Xpetra Ernándes says the *Bolom Chon* are all the different varieties of *wayhel*: tigers, chickens, possums, the animal kingdom in general. For Robert M. Laughlin, the *Bolom Chon* is a velvet ant. For musician Xun Calixta, *Bolom Chon*—which literally means "Tiger Snake"—should be translated as Dancing Tiger. María Gutiérrez says she has no idea how to translate *Bolom Chon*; Munda Tostón finds a sexual connotation for this lame serpent that grows long and shrinks up:

Stand up, Papa.
Stand up, Mama.

Climb on, Papa.
Climb on, Mama.

María Tzu concludes *Bolom Chon* doesn't mean anything at all; it's just the name of a drinking song the Fathermothers made up when the world was created so people could have fun at the fiesta, stomping their feet on the surface of the Earth.

DRINKING WITH FRIENDS is considered one of the greatest of life's pleasures. Men and women consume barrels of sweet cane *chicha* in the fiesta and eighteen-liter jugs of *pox*, moonshine rum distilled in the Chiapas hills. Most non-Protestants consume an alcoholic drink or two every day as part of some ritual. To ask a favor or to borrow money, a drink of *pox* is offered. If you accept the shot, it means you are willing to help out your friend. A lone drinker is just about as rare as an abstainer.

During a curing ceremony, liquor is served to each person present in a tiny gourd cup or a *kurus bis*—one of those small glasses that veladora candles come in, the kind with a cross on the front. If you don't want to drink too much, you say politely, "Just up to the cross, please." One person pours the *pox* and passes the glass; each person drinks in turn, swallowing the firewater in one gulp. "The gourd is empty," you say while handing the glass back to the drink server. In a fiesta, women exchange toasts and couplets, ceremoniously thanking everyone present for each drink:

> I'll take it, Mother of Boiled Corn,
> I will drink it all down.
>
> I'll take it, Father in Charge of Fireworks.
> To the bottom of the gourd!
> —*Mikaela Moshán Culej*

Rum lubricates the gears of society, but alcoholism becomes a plague. When a drinker dies, his friends are obliged to consume all the *pox* the dead man left in his house; otherwise the deceased would suffer a never-ending hangover. The mourners bring several of their own bottles along, burials have been known to turn into serial wakes.

On the last day of the Fiesta of Santa Katarina of Pantelhó, the plaza resembles a battleground. Men and women sprawl unconscious wherever they downed their last toast, their lips moving in silent songs.

THOUGH THE TZOTZILS RECITE POETRY every day, the language of their poems is not colloquial. The vocabulary of the *Incantations* is very old. To understand Tzotzil ritual poetry we were obliged to consult bilingual dictionaries made by colonial friars, contemporaries of Shakespeare

and Cervantes. As Loxa Jiménes explains, "We don't understand it all now, but it forms a part of our flesh and we dream it every night."

Neoliberalism has left its mark on the world and on language; today Tzotzil women pray so their *Pexi Kola* will sell, and so they won't have to look for work as illegal immigrants in the USA.

> Take into account, *Kajval,*
> how much you are going to give me.
>
> I don't want to go to Los Angeles.
> I don't want to work in Florida.
>   —*Xunka' Utz'utz' Ni'*

There are more than a million Mayans now living in the States, many of whom still remember how the Fathermothers of Yucatán spoke when they dictated the incantations of the *Ritual de los Bacabes* to friars in the seventeenth-century:

> Through writing we know
> the origins of the word.
>
> The glyphs will give us the answer.
> How will it be said?
>
> Glyphs of the skies.
> Glyphs of the clouds.
>
> Orange Sun,
> Orange Moon.

Scholars who decipher Mayan glyphs say they were written originally in *Ch'ol*, a language spoken today by neighbors of the Tzotzil. Linguist Kathryn Josserand finds a likeness between the ritual language of the present-day *Ch'ol* and the couplets the Fathermothers carved on the stones of Palenque.

The First Father raised the Pillar of the Sky
and set the stars to spin.

Another world was born.
Venus touched the Earth.

This is how the blood of the First Mother began,
Creator of the Gods and Queen of Palenque.
　　　　　—Temple of the Cross, Palenque

The glyphs speak to our eyes when we see a little hand or a jaguar carved on the stones.
Some glyphs have voices; their sounds go into the ear and tell us the words.

The corresponding glyphs,
the ones that went together,
separated,
from this came
incantations of the saliva.
　　　　　—Ritual de los Bacabes

The poetic word of ritual is discreet, it covers its face with metaphors; this is the secret language of *Zuyua* as defined by ancient Mayan seers in the *Books of Chilam Balam*:

My son, bring me three rays from the sun;
I wish to eat them.

Let it be,
Oh father!

What he is asking for is Sacab, a corn drink with no lime. The language of Zuyua is for praying
for what one wants. Poetry is the food of the gods. According to the ancient Maya book the
Popol Vuh, human beings were created so they would nourish the gods with poetry:

To the Grandmother of the Day:
To the Conjurer of Dawn:

To the Diviner:
To the Soothsayer:

We need to find,
we need to discover

how we are going to create,
how we are going to make

beings who will nourish
and sustain us,

invoke
and venerate us,

when there is light
when there is day.

Our recompense will be the song.
Our recompense will be the word.
    —Popol Vuh

Poet Ernesto Cardenal writes that:

Adam in paradise spoke in verse, according to an ancient Islamic tradition. Poetry
is the first language of humanity...In ancient Greece even the laws were written
in verse; many so-called primitive people know only verse. Poetry seems to be the
most natural form of language.

All over the world the First Fathermothers of humanity produced great works of literature in verse, among which are the *Epic of Gilgamesh*, the *Mahabharata* and the *Navajo Night Chant*. According to Jerome Rothenberg, the first peoples of the American continents:

> created a poetry as diverse as the peoples themselves. As classic for its times & places as Homer was for Europe or the *Book of Songs* for China. Rooted in oral tradition & the potentialities of human voice and presence.

Before there was writing, poems were chanted over and over, generation after generation, so they would not be forgotten. Each singer adds something from her own harvest. The song is polished in the flowing of the years and tongues.

The Tzotzil incantations are characterized by an endless chain of couplets that spirals towards *Kajval*. The complete text of any of these songs would fill several volumes; we could not include every word.

The seers never tire of singing. They endure fiestas that last three days and nights. They climb the path of the holy mountain to toast each cave, at every spring. They follow the wanderings of the *wayhel* with their song. They herd the souls, address the Moon, sweep the sky with their voices so the Sun can drive across the heavens. The words gather the clouds together and awaken the rain. The voices fill the cooking pots and charm the harp.

My goal as translator was to recreate—in another language—poetry as beautiful and fresh as the original. Both the Spanish and the English versions of the texts were translated directly from the Tzotzil. Some concepts—*Kajval, Pukuj, Kaxail, wayhel, Potzlom*—and plant names—*tukum, xjuj, konkon*—for which I could find no equivalent, were left untranslated. The Mayan metaphors were respected; the syntax, metric and titles are my own. These are not line-by-line translations, but renderings of magic. Echoes from the eye of the universe call the bird of our heart. From the womb of song the seers come to life.

Elder Brother of Writing:
Elder Brother of Painting:

Let my animal spirit live
many years
in the pages
of the Book,
in its letters,
its paintings,
on the whole surface
of the Earth.
                    —Manwela Kokoroch

I AM A WOMAN MY WOMAN

I am a woman, my woman.
I am a girl, my girl.

I am woman, the woman.
I am girl, the girl.

I know how to work.
My feet work.
My hands know.

I am girl, my girl.
I am woman, my woman.

You made me woman.
You gave me woman.

Woman of the Flowers.
Mother of the Sky.

Woman of the Roses.
Girl of the Roses.

Flowery Woman of the Roses.
Daughter of the Rose in Bloom.

You gave me woman.
You gave me girl.

You took a girl out of me.
You took a woman out of me.

Woman of the Silk *Huipil*.
Girl of the Silk *Huipil*.

Woman of the Wool *Huipil*.
Girl of the Wool *Huipil*.

I am a girl, my girl.
I am a woman, my woman.

You gave me my spirit.
You gave me my death.
You put my soul inside.

I am the Woman of the Spider *Huipil*.
I am the Girl of the Spider *Huipil*.

Woman of the Bromelia Flower.
Woman of the *Kilon* Flower.

The Moon is full.
The woman in bloom.

My girl, my girl.
My woman, my woman.

Put into my head,
give me in my heart

your three needles,
your three looms,

your gourds,
the tips of your spindles.

I am a girl, my girl.
I am a woman, my woman
—*Loxa Jiménes Lópes*

THE BONESETTER'S SONG

The Sun will have his sunbeams on when they come.
The Sun will be way up in the sky
when the Butterfly Women, the Butterfly Men,
the Women of the Arrows, the Men of the Arrows,
the Hurricane Women, the Whirlwind Men
come with thirteen flowered gourds,
with thirteen lacquered calabash,
to shake this pain out of my bones.

I offer you a red hen.
I sacrifice a gray dove for you,
in the mouth of the cave, at the edge of your table,
inside your house, in the eighth room,
on the twelfth floor,
on the thirteenth step, *Kajval*.

Kindly untie the knots
and patch up things inside the bones
and within the tendons
so that the pain in the marrow
disappears as quickly as a rainbow cloud.
Pain: jump out!
Get lost in the thirteen mountains,
the thirteen hill tops,
inside thirteen stones,
in the heart of the thirteen trees,
in thirteen valleys of the peaks on the horizon.
  —Pasakwala Kómes

SO THE BAT WON'T BITE THE SHEEP

There is a bat, *Kajval*,
a black butterfly
who comes on the wind
and eats the ears of your sheep.

This snake butterfly animal, *Kajval*,
Makes the wool red with blood.
Blood on the back,
blood on its side.
It bites the heart, *Kajval*.

Close his eyes with six pitch pines.
Blind him with incense smoke
so he can't find your sheep,
so he won't bite the little ones just starting to grow.

Block the path of the bat.
Put him away in your cave
in the heart of the rock.
Hide him inside the mountain.
Let him vanish into the weeds, *Kajval*.

It's because of envy
that he bites our blood.
Block the road from the high places, *Kajval*,
stop the moth, stop the bat.
    —*María Tzu*

THE MOTHER OF TREASURE

The Mother of Treasure appears on Tuesday, Thursday and Saturday.
You can see her among the morning stars as a long blue snake.
Her light falls from the sky drawn by the magnet of buried gold.

We don't know where she comes from,
if she comes out of the hills or from the Sun,
but close up she looks like an *atole* pot that glows blue.
She is also a serpent and if she smells the pulse of your fear,
she will bite you when you touch her gold.

There are people who find Treasure and buy a truck.
I myself have seen her blue light fall nearby.
There's a piece of cornfield where nothing will grow, next to my son's house.
You'll ask me why I don't go out at night to look for gold there.
But I am afraid of demons, and if you are afraid,
you won't find anything, even if you dig three meters down.

There's nothing left to do but hire a seer
to talk to our Sun so he'll make me rich.
In order to pray, however, you have to fast for three days,
and since I'm starving to death anyway, I could never take that.

I work hard, and work makes me hunger, you see.
It's because of my poverty that I'll never be rich.
My lack of everything scares the Mother of Treasure away.
    —Xunka' Utz'utz' Ni'

TO KAXAIL

I step and walk
on your flowering face,

Holy Mother, Holy Wildwood,
Sacred Earth, Sacred Ground.

Show me the way, Mother,
put me on the right track.

Rise up, Holy Rock!
Rise up, Holy Tree!

Come with me on the way up.
Be with me on the way down.

Sacred Mother,
Holy Breast,

Holy *Kaxail*,
Sacred Earth,

Holy Ground,
Holy Soil,

Sacred *Ahau*,
Holy Snake,

Holy Thunderbolt:
Protect me with your shadow.
　　　　　—Maruch Méndes Péres

PLANTING A TREE

Sacred Tree,
Holy Pine:

I am going to plant you
in the Sacred Earth.

Take my gift:
these three grains of corn

that I'll bury at your foot,
beneath your branches

to pay you back
for your help.

I'll tie my loom to you.
I'll weave in your shade.

My chickens will roast in your branches.
Birds will sleep in your crown.

Climb up, grow tall,
Sacred Tree, Holy Pine.
                —*Xpetra Ernándes*

WITCHCRAFT FOR ATTRACTING A MAN

I want him to come with flowers in his heart.
With all his heart,

I want him to talk to my body.
I want his blood to ache for me
when he sees me on the way to the market.

I want his mother to come to my house to ask for me
with her head bowed down
and a jug of booze for my dad.

I want him to come on a new road
so his white clothes won't get dirty.

I don't want him to fall in the mud.
Don't let the bad snake bite him.

Look into his eyes, *Kajval*.
I'm telling you this to your nose, to your ears:
His name is Xtumin.

I've spoken to your head.
I've spoken to your bones.
I called you with my mouth.

I want to join myself to him.
I want this man to be my other half.
    —*Xpetra Ernándes*

SO THE DOG WON'T BARK AT MY BOYFRIEND

Shut the dog's mouth for me.
Lock his snout

with a key,
with a padlock.

Close his eyes.
Stop up his ears

with twelve candles, *Kajval*,
and a bottle of firewater.

Tie up his paw,
Tie up his other paw.

Make him curl up on the ground.
Make him go to sleep.

Walk ahead of my boyfriend.
Blow on him with your breath

so the dog can't smell his tracks,
so the dog won't sniff his hands.

Don't let
the dog bark.

Don't let
the mutt bite, *Kajval.*
         —*Xpetra Ernándes*

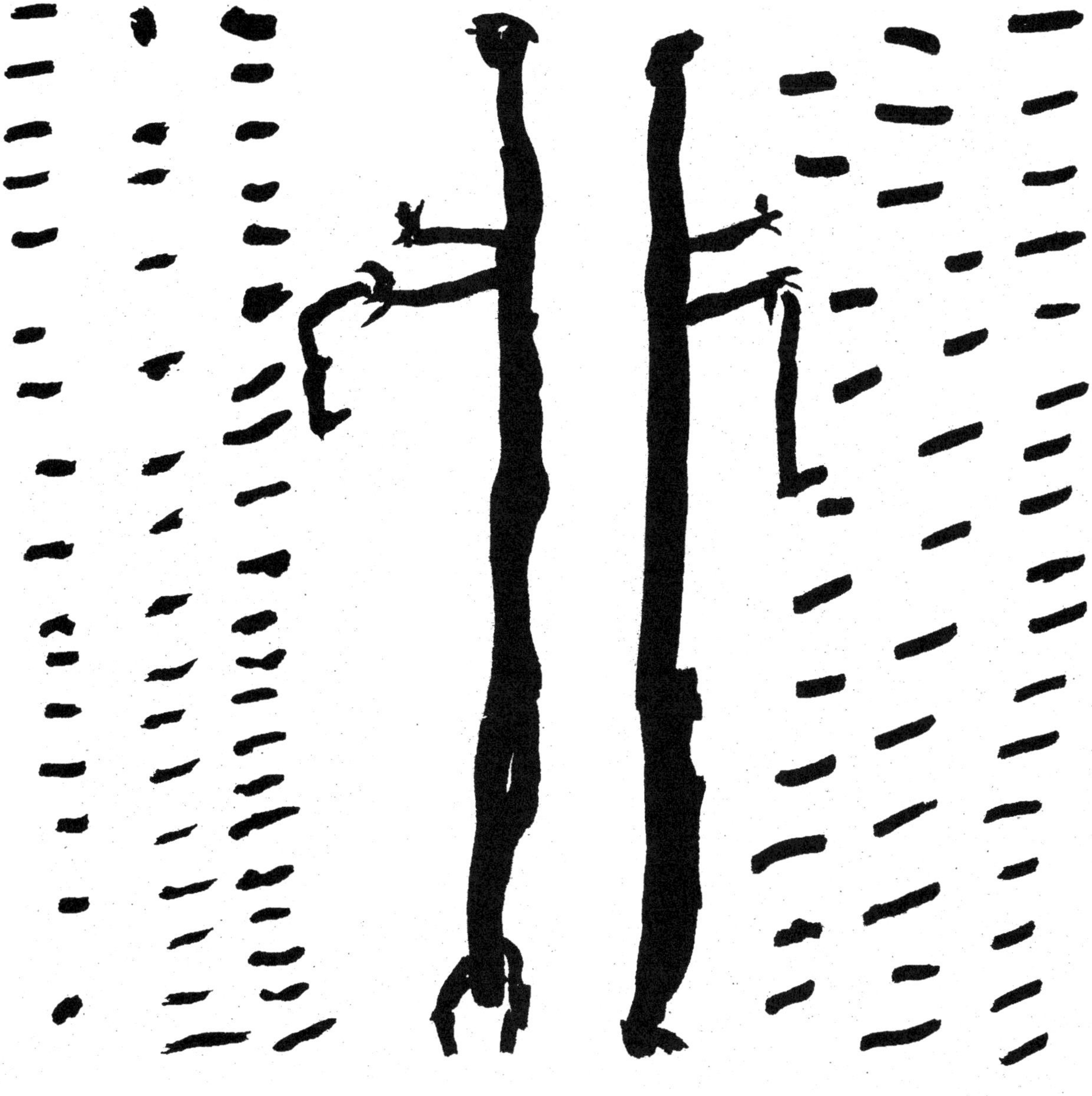

TO PLANT THE EARTH

I'm going to dig a hole in your face, Holy Earth.
Holy Sky, I'm hoeing into your body.

To bury your holy body,
I'm going into your flesh.

I'm planting my cornfield.
Planting my work.

Half my fathers,
half my mothers,

hold in their hands,
carry on their backs

something that is alive,
something that is complete.

Their nets are filled,
their bags have stuff inside.

Their gunnysacks look heavy
when they carry them around.

I'm gong to hoe your face.
I'm going into your body.

I want you to fill my gourd, Holy Earth.
I want you to fill my bean pot, Sacred Sky.
      —Jwana te la Krus Posol

TO THE BLUE JAY

Blue Jay, Blue Jay:
Sacred Bird:

Don't starve me to death.
Don't eat my corn, don't pull up the beans.

It's all I have to eat.
All I have to drink.

Here's your corn
in these four new gourds
in front of the house,

in the corners of my yard
for you to play with.

Eat only what's yours
so there will be enough left for me to eat

with my children,
with my husband.

I won't hurt you, Blue Jay.
I'm not scolding you,

Sacred Animal,
Holy Bird.

I'm giving you some of my corn and beans.
This is your food.
Come and get it.
—*Antonia Moshán Culej*

PRAYER SO MY MAN WON'T HAVE TO CROSS THE LINE

Take into account, *Kajval*,
that I am speaking to you.

I bring you smoke.
I offer you flowers.

Take into account, *Kajval*,
what you are going to give me.

The others have horses.
They have sheep.

They have hens.
Trucks.

Take into account, *Kajval*,
how much you are going to give me.

I don't want to work on a plantation.
I don't want to go to someone else's house.
I don't want to work far away.

I don't want to go to Los Angeles.
I don't want work in Florida.
                —*Xunka' Utz'utz' Ni'*

SONG FOR THE RAIN

I'll kneel for as long as it takes.
I'll stretch myself out before you on the ground,
Father Thunder, Mother Thunder.
My cornfields are suffering. The corn is drying up, *Kajval.*
Hunger gnaws us with its dry mouth.

Make the Earth green.
Let the *milpa* flower.
Put something into our mouths,
even if it's just a bean, just a pea.
At least a lima bean, a pumpkin, or a turnip leaf.

Let water fall from your eyes,
Father of the White Mountain, Mother of the White Cave,
Lord of the Snake,
He Who Has His Belly Full of Serpents,
He Who Eats Jaguars.

Make all the clouds from all the lands come together.
Make the rain work on the whole Earth.
We want water from your three sacred wells, *Kajval.*

We don't want wind.
We don't want lightning.
Nor roaring thunder, nor hail.

Just water, *Kajval,*
to wet the dust,
to end this drought that bites us.
             —*María Xila*

AGAINST THE RAINBOW

The rainbow bites me, *Kajval*.
Now she's spying on me.

Chasing me
into the house.

Get her out of here!
Run her off, *Kajval*!

Throw rocks at her.
Spit three tobaccos at her.

She's nothing but the Mother of Evil.
She eats my heart out.

Don't let her boss me around.
Don't let that *Pukuj* pick fights.
   —María Tzu

WORDS TO BRING DOWN FEVER

Sacred Pine Tree,
Holy Mirror:
Fill my mouth with verses.
Let my words have life,
for raising the sick,
for bringing down the fever,
with thirteen chamomile flowers
with thirteen *tukum* flowers.

My words are roses.
The rose speaks in my mouth.

I am nine pine branches.
I am mountain palm.
I am nine *xjuj*,
nine *konkon*.

Sacred pine, Holy mirror:
Kindly bring the fever down.
Untie it from the body.
Do your best.

Don't turn your back on my words.
I've suffered enough.
I've called the soul,
to your face,

in your sacred visage,
Holy Mirror, *Kajval.*
                    —Pasakwala Kómes

FOR THE HARP

Sacred Music,
Holy Harp:

Here's a little nip
to lighten your heart.

I'm going to play you
so you will sing.

I want you to enjoy the fiesta.
Let your heart be happy.

Flowers in your head,
in your heart,
in your blood.

I'm going to pluck your strings:
strum strum.

We drink and sing.
We are dancing.

Having a good time!
Let our hearts flower!

OK, Sacred Music,
Holy Harp,

forgive me for playing you.
Thank you, Sacred Harp.
             —*Xpetra Ernándes*

THE SAINT KEEPERS' SONG

Your musicians are assembled.
Your incense burners have come.

Your flower bearer is here,
the man who serves the drinks,

the women who make the tortillas.
All your children are gathered together.

Your harp sings.
Your rattles are happy.

We are overjoyed.
Your flowered face is shining white, *Kajval.*
   —María Patixtán Likán Chitom

THE BOLOM CHON

Dancing Tiger in the sky.
Dancing Tiger on the Earth.

Keeper of the sky.
Keeper of the Earth.

You have a limp, Dancing Tiger.
You have a long foot, *Bolom Chon.*

Your beard is fluffy, Dancing Tiger.
Your beard is long, *Bolom Chon.*

Rise up, Father.
Rise up, Mother.

Stand tall, Papa.
Stand tall, Mama.

Step up, Papa.
Climb on, Mama.

We like each other on the Earth.
We fall in love here in the sky.
       —*Rominka Vet*

A TOAST

I'll take it, Mother of Boiled Corn,
I'll drink it all down.

I'll take it, Father in Charge of Fireworks.
To the bottom of the gourd!

So let's drink
the way *Kajval* has shown us.

The gods have ordered us to drink.
Is this not true?

Yes, *"Umm up yaya,"* we say at times,
Kajval showed us this also.

I have drunk now, it's all gone.
There is nowhere to get more.

There's not even a nickel to buy any.
All gone, all gone.

"Upa ya ya," we say:
Hope we don't fall down in the street.

For sure, God willing,
Oh God, don't let us fall down, right?

Right.
All gone, all gone.
                    —*Mikaela Moshán Culej*

THE DRUNKEN WOMAN'S SONG

Saint Mother,
Godmother, I am drunk.

I caught the drops that fall from your roof.
I drank your shadow.

Now I am getting drunk.
Anyway, my Saint Mother,
anyway, my Godmother,

look after me
so I won't trip over something.

I am drunk; I have drunk,
my Saint Mother, my Godmother,
Saint Maruch, *Niña* Maruch.

I want all your pretty ones to overwhelm me.
I want to sing,

Virgin Maruch,
Niña Maruch.

I am a drinker of drink.
I drank your wine.

It has gone to my head.
My heart is spinning.

I know how to drink.
I know how to drink everything.
     —Maruch Méndes Péres

CALLING THE DEAD TO SUPPER

Dead Father:
Dead Mother:

Open your graves,
open your eyes.

Come rest your hearts.
Come rest your blood.

Your celebration is ready.
We are burning pitch pines

to light your way
to our house.

Come eat with us.
Come drink with us.

Have a little *atole*,
a few tortillas.

Here's a shot of the rum you like
to keep your eyes open.

We don't see each other anymore,
nor can we talk,

nor eat together every day as we used to
on the surface of the Earth.
                    —*María Álvares Jiménes, Me' Avrila*

HOW THE MOON TAUGHT US TO WEAVE

Long ago women made threads as today we make our children:
They spun them with the strength of their bodies.
When the Earth began, they say, the Moon climbed a tree.
There she was weaving, there she was spinning, up in the tree.
"Learn to weave!" she said to the First Fathermothers.
"Learn to spin!" That's how weaving began.

The Moon had her carding combs, her loom, and a spindle.
I don't know if she had sheep up in the tree
or if it was the silk from the flowers she spun.

The Moon cut branches off the tree to form her loom.
She had her stick to measure the thread, her *komen*
which was very long and stuck out of the top of the tree.
Before dawn she was up in the tree weaving,
working the white of the blouse, the red seeds in the brocade.
This is how our ancestors learned.

The Moon climbed to the top of the tree. She kept going up
her *komen* like it was a ladder, she climbed into the sky.
Or maybe she jumped, swinging in the branches.

We still have the loom she left us, and her clothes in old coffers.
The stewards take care of them. During the fiesta
they put incense on the dresses the Moon wore
when the Earth was new.
They are so grand!
No one could weave them today.
   —Loxa Jiménes Lópes

TO ENCHANT THE SPINDLE

Holy Spindle,
do your work.
Whirling, twirling,
dancing in your gourd.

Don't get angry,
please don't scold me.
Let us work together
with one heart

to spin the yarn to weave my blankets,
the warp for wool skirts,

the fine thread for *huipils*
to wear in the fiesta,

the thick weft of black ponchos,
and warm white cloaks.

Brown thread for belts and shawls,
red for tortilla bags,

men's shirts,
women's blouses,

baby clothes,
and diapers.

Thank you for your help,
Sacred Spindle, Holy Whorl.
   —Xpetra Ernándes

LEARNING TO DYE WOOL

Woman in Flower:
Mother in Bloom:

Your first daughters,
the first of your daughters

want to weave their shawls,
weave their blankets

so they won't feel the frost,
so they won't feel the rain.

Tire yourself in the teaching.
Put into their heads, into their hearts,
into their hands,

your three spindles,
the first three carding combs,

the first three dye pots,
the first three dyes,

the three branches of bitter herb,
the three bundles of dodder,
the three leaves of *ch'i te'*.

Show me your three books,
your three letters,
the ink of the letters.

Teach your daughters, Lady Wildwood,
Coffer Where the Secrets Are Kept.
　　　　—María Tzu

A GIRL'S SONG ABOUT A TANGLED LOOM

I want to be as pretty as you,
Mother Moon, Mother Sky.

Give me your spindle,
give me your loom!

I need your fine needle,
and your ten fingers, too.

My little loom is tangled!
My work is ruined!

iiiiiiiii! uuuuuu!
My loom is destroyed.

Ay, Mother Moon,
Ay, Sacred Godmother:

My loom is tangled up!
My weaving is ruined!

My Moon,
Woman in Flower,

Mother of the Flowers,
Girl of the Flowers:

Make me smart like you!
Show me how to fix my loom.
                    —*María Patixtán Likán Chitom*

ASKING FOR HER HAND

Mother of the groom:

As all the daughters of woman,
all the sons of man,
since my father's been around,
since my mother started things,
long before the ancient ones
had white hair,
I come humbly, mud falling from my feet,
—pardon the dust on my hands—
to take the honey from your mouths,
to steal your gift, your pain,
your Image of the Goddess.

A man cannot live alone.
A woman cannot live alone.

Mother of the bride:

You can see with your eyes of Earth,
on the face of the Earth
how they fit together,
how they complete each other.
Four hands, four feet.

Our sons and daughters will come to no good
if they elope together,
if they scold each other, hit one another.
We'll give them advice
when the Sun comes up,
when the Sun is on high,
when the Sun's face melts in flower.
                    —*Markarita Váskes Kómes*

BEFORE FELLING A TREE

Don't kill me, don't fall on me,
Sacred Tree, Sacred Pine.
It's because I am in need
that I cut you down,
Sacred Oak, Sacred Vine,
Holy Earth,
Holy Sky.

Give me your firewood, your kindling,
your torchlight so I can see what I'm eating, *Kajval.*
Give me your heat to bake my tortillas, to boil my beans.
Give me the beams to build my house
and pillars to support the thatch, the vines, the mud.

Kaxil, Godmother:
I'm going to split your wood, your arms, your legs,
your face, your head.
I'm going to chop you down with my ax,
with my machete.
Don't scold me, don't drip your tears on me.
I don't want to cut you down, but it's cold.
I want a fire to keep warm.
I'm hungry, I have to make tortillas,
I need light to see at night
so I can grind my corn,
so I can boil my hominy and beans.

Kajval, give me your pitch pine.
Your sunbeams for my candles.
Thanks to you, I'm still alive.
                    —*Antonia Moshán Culej*

TO THE WILDWOOD

Sacred Mother,
Holy Woman in Flower:
Wildwood, Sacred Pine, Holy Oak:
I'm going to build my house.
I must chop you down
and raise you up as my house post
so I'll have a place to sleep.
I'm going to daub my walls with your body.
Don't scold me, don't be angry,
don't fly off the handle, get hot under the collar.
Let us be of one heart when you give yourself to me.
Sacred Mother, Holy Coffer Where the Secrets Are Kept:
I'm going to stand on your face.
I'm going to walk on you, Holy Mother Breast.
I am so poor.
I need to plaster my house with your mud, your earth.
Give me your body to make my walls
to keep the rain out, the mist, the frost, Holy Mother.
Otherwise Mother *Pukuj* will eat me,
Woman of the Woods will frighten me,
Monster With Its Feet on Backwards will come to visit,
along with Boogey Man With a Hat Like a Griddle,
Charcoal Cruncher, Meat Stripper,
and snake, jaguar,
coyote, fox,
owl, night hummingbird, bat.

Holy Mother, Sacred Wildwood, I need your tree, your oak,
so I'll have a place to live where I'm not afraid.
   —*Xpetra Ernándes*

SO THE NEW HOUSE WON'T EAT US

My house is built,
my hearth is made,
Three Sacred Mothers,
Holy Earth, *Kaxil*.

We are going to live here.
We are going to sit here.
We are going to shit here.
We are going to pee here
beneath your flowering face,
each day, beneath your flowery eyes.

I am touching the ground with my forehead
as I say this, *Kajval*.

We are going to sleep here.
We are going to rest here.
We are going to sin here
and make love.

I hope your heart won't scold us,
that your blood doesn't nag us,
that nightmares don't disturb our sleep here,
nor witchcraft.

The neighbors claim we are rich, *Kajval*,
but we have no treasures.
Close the mouths of the envious
so they can't gossip about us.

Let the saints in their coffers,
the voices that speak from inside old chests,
stand up for those who live in this house.

Protect us from being eaten by a vine or a stick.
Save us from being devoured by the new thatch
or the shiny nails.

Here is your food, *Kaxil*.
Dinner is served.
Eat this meat
instead of the bodies of your children.

We offer you gifts, *Kaxil*.
Something for the red envy that bites our hearts:

A little pig, *Kajval*,
so the new house
won't eat the people in it.
        —*Xunka' Utz'utz' Ni'*

BORROWING A GOURD

For your life,
please help me.

Lend me your gourd,
your bowl.

I come from a lowly place,
I am falling down

from work, serving my people.
I bow my head.

My shadow falls on your hands,
lies at your feet,

Holy Woman,
Sacred Lady.
                —*María Álvarez Jiménes, Me' Avrila*

TO RETURN A CEREMONIAL HUIPIL

Ladies and Gentlemen:

You are sitting here in the road,
squatting in life's way.

I have come to put at your feet,
to place in your hands

the clothes that served me.
The weaving you lent me.

I thank you for your generosity.
You were kind to me.

Let us drink a toast now.
I have my *cargo*, I am drunk.
                    —María Álvarez Jiménes, Me' Avrila

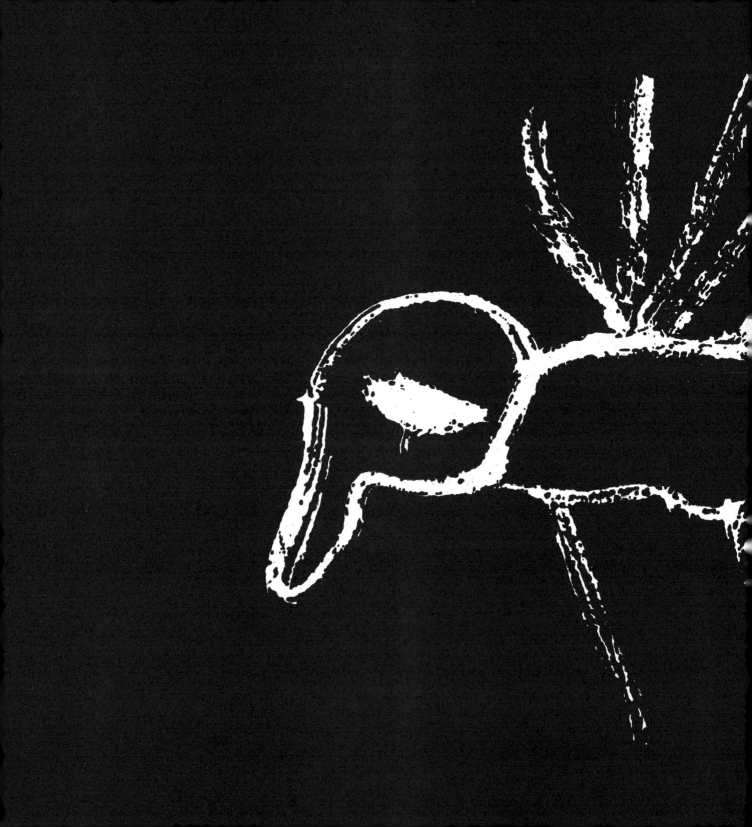

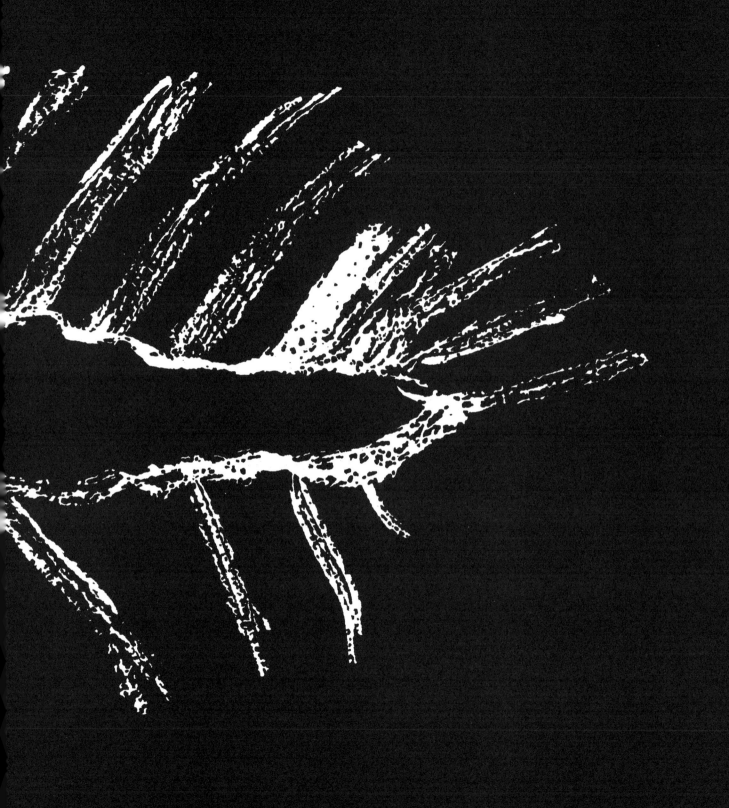

AGAINST THE HUMMINGBIRD WHO SINGS AT NIGHT

We are going to have a talk now, *Kajval.*
We are kneeling down to say the words

so the hummingbird
won't take away our health,

so our husband
won't die, *Kajval.*

I don't want to lose my child, *Kajval.*
I don't want

this flying snake, *Kajval,*
to carry off my gift.

Hide it somewhere.
Get it out of here.

It's up to you, *Kajval.*
You created the hummingbird,

you made the owl that sings in the night.
Get them going

down the road, *Kajval,*
before they carry off my corpse.

It's in your hands, *Kajval,*
you're the boss.
      —María Tzu

DURING THE ECLIPSE

My Father is dying on the face of the Sky, *Kajval*.
We are frightened in our hearts.

Your flowery eye is shut, Father.
The flower of your face is hidden.

The light went black, *Kajval*.
The Earth is dark.

We can't tell if dawn will come back
to the sky.

Something is devouring,
something is destroying, *Kajval*.

We beg you to give us back your fire.
Today, *Kajval*.

May your light never diminish.
May your grandeur never end.

We are crying for your sake, *Kajval*.
We are counting the beats of our hearts.
Our hearts are remembering you.

My husband is crying, my children, his children.
The big and the little.
The newly born.
              —*Petú Xantis Xantis*

A MIDWIFE ADDRESSES THE NEWBORN

When you grow up,
when you can speak,
you will work in the cornfield,
you will earn money
to buy your salt,
to buy your chile
when you are hungry, when you are thirsty.

This is your tumpline
to help you with your burden
when you gather kindling
for the fire
to keep you warm,
to cook your food,
to boil the water.

This is your machete
for chopping wood
when you light a fire
to make you warm, to heat your food.

This is your weaving stick
for earning your pay.

This is your spindle
for you to spin, for your work.
to get money to buy your food.

This is your comb
for you to comb your hair.
                    —*Rosa Xulemhó*

LULLABY

Go to sleep little baby, go to sleep.
Your daddy's drunk

and if he hits me,
I'm running to the woods.

Go to sleep little baby, go to sleep.
If you cry, the *Pukuj* will come.

Here he comes now.
Devil's coming.
Your daddy's the *Pukuj*.
                    —*Petra Tzon Te' Vitz*

FOR A FRIGHTENED CHILD WHO CANNOT SLEEP

Lord of the Toadstools,
Lady of the Toadstools,
Patron of the Sacred Jaguar,
Keeper of the Holy Chair of Our Soul,
Guardian of Where the Animals Spirits Are Kept:

This little girl fell down,
she was frightened in your face, on your Earth, *Kajval*.
The little woman's soul
is being held somewhere.

Untie her with an herb,
a weed, *Kajval*.
I want thirteen of your pills,
because something has happened;
she can't fall asleep, she won't lie down.
My little baby can't dream.

Bring her back
with pine cones,
with wild berries,
and candles of many colors.
Let her come with her flowers blooming,
with flowers in her body,
Holy Mother Breast,
Sacred Earth,
Ancient Coffer Where the Secrets Are Kept.
　　　　　—Petú Bak Bolom

FOR A DEAD CHILD

Little dead one,
my gift,

my suffering,
my son,

my ear of corn
just beginning to grow

on this leaf of Earth,
in this leaf of Sky.

Mother in Flower,
Mother of What Is Difficult:

Make me forget,
take him out of my heart.

Let little Mario be gone from my memory,
Flowering Mother of the Sky.
   —Loxa Jiménez Lópes

SO THE BABY WILL LEARN TO SPEAK

Here's your little tortilla
with three holes in it

so you will learn to speak,
so your mouth will be opened,

so you will talk
and laugh.

Come here, child,
take your tortilla.

Peer through
the crack in the door.

See the face on it?
This hole is its mouth.

See the eyes?
Take it with your lips.

Eat your birdfeed.
You'll chatter like a parrot.
— *Antonia Moshán Culej*

A GIRL'S SONG ABOUT A WILD DEER

How do you dance,
wild deer?

We are red fawns,
we are gray fawns.

Leaping in the forest,
walking in the valley.

We will catch fireflies
to light your way at night

when you travel to Guatemala
to bring fireworks for the Rain God.

Little deer:
you are my soul's companion.

Hide yourself in the cave,
inside the clouds.

Don't let the jaguar get you,
don't be killed by a bullet.
            —*Verónika Taki Vaj*

SONG OF A SHEPHERDESS

Eat, my brown lambs,
my spotted sheep.

Let's go to the woods,
among the oaks where everything is green.

Little lambs from far away
on the other side of the sea:

Come with me to the woods,
to the oaks.

Let's go find your food,
your green grass,

my little sheep,
my *mimi*,

my *kaxlanes*,
my pintos, my brown ones.

Let's go to the woods, to the caves
to look for *pitz'otz'* berries,

we'll find your *kulch'ix* leaves,
your *k'amiltajte'*,

my little sheep,
my little girls,
the smallest of my daughters.
    —María Patixtán Likan Chitóm

TO STOP MOTHER WIND

Where the Wind walks, *Kajval*,
hunger is here to stay.

The Wind knocks down the *milpa*.
She has a scarlet heart,

she's an envious thief
who steals our corn on the cob.

My cornfield
is not the Wind's dinner, *Kajval*!

Stop the Wind.
Stop the Cloud.

And if the Wind comes anyway,
send her around the back of the cornfield,

off to one side
of your sacred body, *Kajval*.

If the aphid comes,
stop it in its tracks.

If there is a Mother of Aphids,
or a Father of Aphids,

send them to another hill,
to another valley, *Kajval*.

What am I to eat if there is no food, Father?
My heart is so used to eating only corn, *Kajval*.
        —*Petú Bak Bolom*

FOR MARUCH VET, SOLD TO A CAVE

Mother of the Night,
Father of the Night,
Great Star of Venus,
Mother Month,
Mother Moon:

Get up, *Kajval*!
Put on your best clothes.
Let Maruch Vet's body
out of where she's scared to death,
sold to a cave,
sold to a mountain.

OK, *Kajval*,
our word, our prayer
is here before you
inside your cave.
We offer you these feathers,
this dove in exchange for Maruch Vet, *Kajval*.

A little food for you, a little drink,
Guardian of the Sacred Cave:
Keeper of the Holy Mountain:

Let go of her body.
It's tied up, shut in,
getting skinnier every day inside the hill, *Kajval*.

This burden of hers
isn't getting any lighter, *Kajval*.
        —*Antel Péres Ok'il*

DRINKING WITH THE DEAD

Well, let's drink
a little

of this head hottener,
this heart heater.

Take your shot
to the bottom of the glass!

If you get drunk,
if you drink liquor,

take along a candle,
so you can see where you're going, OK?

Don't fall down on the way,
don't get lost.
                    —*María Álvares Jiménes, Me' Avrila*

SO THE LIZARD WON'T EAT THE BEANS

We're dirt poor, *Kajval*,
when our beans won't grow.

This animal, *Kajval*,
this lizard of yours

eats the cornfield
down to the last bean.

The only thing that's left is my hunger, *Kajval*.
Still have that.

It's your fault, *Kajval*, that this lizard is
walking around on Earth and in the sky.

Kajval, Father:
Do this for me.
   —María Tzu

TO THE SOUL OF CORN

Come back from where the raccoon took you,
from where the grackle ate you,

from the mole's tunnel,
the weevil's mouth,

the gopher hole,
the worm's house, the rat's den,

where the water washed you out,
where you drowned inside the Earth.

You never saw daylight.
You didn't grow like the other corn.

Come back from where you are lost,
gather together all your souls of corn.

We are making your fiesta.
We give you food and song.

We serve you
worm-eaten corn and beans.

Sing and be happy,
with guitar and rattle.
                    —*Xpetra Ernándes*

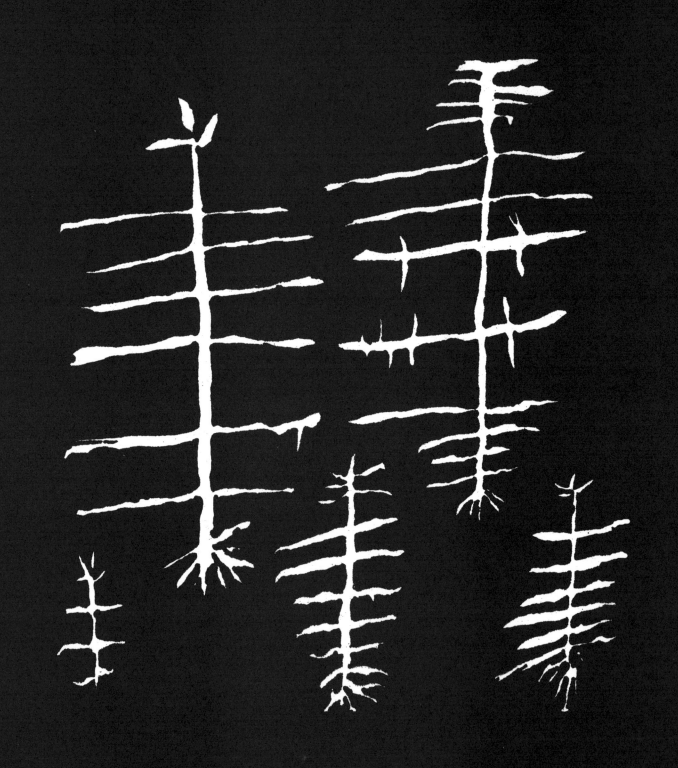

SO THE CORN WILL LAST FOR A WHILE

How much will I harvest, *Kajval?*
How many of your sunbeams?

How much of your body
will I put in my basket, Father?

Let no one take it from me!
Let no one want what I have!

Just you notice, *Kajval,*
how much I bring home
to where I keep my shadow.

I'm going to harvest it slowly.
I'm going to bring it to my house,

and eat it little by little,
so we won't run out of corn so fast.
　　　　　　　　—María Tzu

TO KEEP THE SOLDIERS AWAY

Listen Sacred Thunderbolt:
Listen Sacred Hill:
Listen Sacred Lighting:
Listen Sacred Cave:
We have come to wake up your conscience.
We have come to awaken your heart
so you'll fire your rifle,
so you'll sound your cannon
to block the road from the men
who come in the night,
who come at dawn with their weapons.
Don't let them beat us up.
Don't let them torture us.
Don't let them rape us
in our houses, in our homes.

Great Flowery San Juan:
Lord of the Earth, Guardian of the Sky:
Father Huitepec Hill, Mother Huitepec Hill:
Holy Father White Cave, Holy Mother White Cave:
Holy Father San Cristóbal, Holy Mother San Cristóbal:
Don't let them come into these lands.
Make their rifles freeze up, let their pistols go cold.
Kajval, take this bouquet of flowers.
Accept this offering of leaves,
the smoke from my incense.
Sacred Father Chaklajun, Sacred Mother Chaklajun.
    —Xunka' Utz'utz' Ni'

TEN BLUES OF THE SKY

You have seen me, Ten Holy Heavens,
Ten Blues of the Sky,
Mother Moon, you have watched me.
You have seen I am not stealing,
Mother Moon, Holy Virgin.

Thanks to the strength
of my feet and my hands,
I am eating.
I have tortillas,
I find a bean or two,
a kernel of corn to plant,
I grow pumpkins,
watermelon squash
to eat, to drink.

Sacred Mother Moon:
Holy Virgin:
San Pegro:
Holy Moon:
Father San Mikel, *Kajval*:
You have given me ten ears of corn,
ten kernels, ten beans you have given me,
ten black *tzitz* avocados.
You have put ten ears of corn
into my heart,
because I don't steal, Mother Moon.
            —*Mikaela Moshán Culej*

SO I WON'T HAVE TO STEAL

For the life of me, *Kajval*,
I can't be a thief.
I can't do these things, *Kajval*.

I take each day
only what you give me.

I touch nothing but my needle,
my spindle,
the inner skin of an ancient gourd, *Kajval*.

I live day to day,
an hour at a time.

I don't know how to rob.
I can't seem to learn, *Kajval*.

Don't let it come into my heart.
Don't let it enter my head.
                    —*Loxa Jiménes Lópes*

PEXI KOLA MAGIC

Remind people to buy from me, *Kajval*.
Not from the other store.

Send me customers, *Kajval*.
With lots of cash, *Kajval*.

I want to sell my cigarettes one by one,
crackers, candy, salt.

Make them drink soda pop;
if it stays too long in the cooler,
the bottle caps rust.

Don't let your dew turn sour;
don't let your *Panta* rot, the *Pexi* go bad.

Make soda pop support me
like a son who works to feed his mom.
                    —*Loxa Jiménes Lópes*

THE TALKING BOX SPEAKS

"Are you there?
I'm from the Universe.
I want bread
and half a crate of soda pop.

Are you there, Sons of Man?
Sane as always?
Got a question?
OK, I'm on my way.
Just a minute.
Don't worry.

Rin-Ran-Rin! I'm back.
What was lost can be found.

I'm going to look for it near Venus
and punish the guilty one.
Tipín, tipín, tipín! you'll hear my whip.
Ay, ay, ay! the thief will cry out.
Nothing to be done.
That's destiny.

That'll be fifty pesos.
And a kilo of incense.

See you later,
Sons of Women.
Goodbye,
Defender of the Angels."

     —*María Ernándes Kokov*

POTZLOM

I come with a live dove
to blind the eyes of the dream-borne *Potzlom*.
Butch *Potzlom*,
Girl *Potzlom*,
Red *Potzlom*,
Yellow *Potzlom*,
Black *Potzlom*,
Red Rainbow,
Striped Rainbow,
Cold *Potzlom*,
Fireball *Potzlom*,
I dream a sea.
I dream a whirlpool
tied to the Eye of Rain,
holding on to the Son of Water,
shut up in the cave,
locked in the house of the hearthstone.
I call to the green basalt.
I call to the yellow basalt, the black basalt,
Son of Fire, Son of Wood,
Daughter of the Mountain, Daughter of Ash:
No more falling leaves!
No more pain like a hoe striking clay!
She has forgotten her heart.
She has forgotten her blood.
Unbind the skin of her pulse,
the surface of her bones,
the face of her face.
                    —*Manwela Kokoroch*

POTZLOM

Take away the stabbing pain, the burning
footprints of the Father,
footprints of the Mother,
treading of the Father *Potzlom*,
Red Mother *Potzlom*,
Green Father *Potzlom*,
Green Mother *Potzlom*,
Black Father *Potzlom*,
Black Mother *Potzlom*,
Gold Father *Potzlom*,
Gold Mother *Potzlom*,
Rainbow Fathers,
Rainbow Mothers,
White Gold Fathers,
White Gold Mothers,
Metal Father, Metal Mother,
Alperez Father, *Alperez* Mother,
Clown Fathers, Clown Mothers,
Armadillo Fathers,
Lion Fathers, Lion Mothers,
Jaguar Fathers, Jaguar Fathermothers,
their footprints, their handprints,
the welts their whips make,
the marks their ropes leave,
bruises from their chains, *Kajval*,
scars from their bullets,
from their rifles, from their cannon, *Kajval*.
Do this favor for me, Master Writer
in the heart of the Sky, *Kajval*.
　　　　　　—*María Patixtán Likan Chitóm*

DRINKING AGAIN

I am called the Sacred Woman.
I am called the Sacred Godmother.

I am the Virgin Maruch.
I am the Virgin *Mestiza*.

I am the drunken woman.
I am the drunken girl.

You gave me my drunkenness,
Godmother of the Drunks.

I feel very sweet.
I feel very sour.

This booze tastes like melon.
Like watermelon.

The vapor from the kettle,
the sweat of the coiling snake,
the rum that rinses out the barrel.

My head spins.
My heart is on fire.

You called me the drunken woman, Holy Mother.
You made me a drunken woman, Sacred Godmother.
                    —*Maruch Méndes Péres*

SONG OF THE PLUMED SERPENT

Snake in the Sky,
Snake on the Earth.

Yellow Snake *la la la*.
Green Snake *la la la*.

Painted snake.
Nine painted snakes.

Snake with a windy tail.
Nine snakes with windy tails.

Plumed Serpent on the Earth.
Plumed Serpent in the Sky.

Serpent that guards the corn.
Serpent that protects the woods.

Little snake in the heart of heaven *la la la*.
Little snake in the heart of glory *la la la*.
　　　　　—Loxa Jiménes Lópes

THE WOMAN WITH A MASK OF EARTH

I have my pussy because I am a woman.
Are you going to eat me?
Is your dick big enough, Beast Man?
Dog Food. Buzzard Chow.
Lick my ass, Dog Nose,
Lick my puss.
Eat my shit, Donkey Man.
Are you looking at my asshole?
Don't you have one of your own, man?

They're coming, they're coming! They are killing!
Going to throw my mud to the Devil.
They've got machetes.
AAAAAY! Murderers!
Open your door, Antonio, they are killing me!

If you want to fuck me,
my cunt wants it.
But a big dick.
If it's little, I don't want it.
Defend me, defend me.
They are killing me!
The soldiers are coming! *AAAAAY!*

Protect me from the soldiers.
They are killing me, *AAAAAY!*
I don't want to cover myself in Earth.
I don't want to dress myself in mud.
　　　　　　　—María Kartones

THE XPAKINTÉ

The *Xpakinté* is not really a person,
although she looks like a woman.
She lives in the fog beneath the tall oaks,
under branches hung with lichens and moss.

The *Xpakinté* appears in the night
when the drunks are stumbling home.
They see the face of their wives
on the *Xpakinté*.
She wears pretty red pompons in her braids,
just like a wife.

It's late, says the *Xpakinté*.
Let's go home, honey.

She leads the drunk off down a shortcut.
He follows along blindly until he realizes
he's lost in the thick brush.
The *Xpakinté* takes off her clothes.
He embraces her.
She turns into a hollow tree
full of hairy caterpillars that sting like fire.

The *Xpakinté* is not a person,
but she looks like a woman
when our men are drunk in the woods
near the fog bank
where the oaks grow tall.
                —*Munda Tostón*

HEX TO KILL THE UNFAITHFUL MAN

Let him pay with his flesh, *Kajval*,
by tomorrow or the next day, *Kajval*.
Let thirteen Devil Woman, thirteen Goddesses of Death,
snuff out his name.
Let a wind that starts in his head, in his heart,
blow his candle out.
Let him die in the road.
Let him be run over by a car.
By a bicycle.
Break his leg.
If he dies, I'm going to be laughing.
Stab a knife into his heart.
Nail a nail into his body.
Let a giant termite grow in his navel.
A huge wasp. A fire ant in his ear.
Let his skull be stung
with poison, the nine poisons
of the Four-nosed Serpent.
Toss his soul into the shit pile.
Let worms eat his soul, eat his dick.
Let his belly swell up.
Let him choke on a bean.
Give him diarrhea, dry up his semen.
Make his prick shrivel up.

Don't let him get away.
Grab him.
Kill him in bed.
                    —*Tonik Nibak*

TO THE BEARER OF TIME

Elder Brother of Writing:
Elder Brother of Painting:
I've come with roses, with lilies,
carnations and chamomile.

Lend me your ten masks
so my years within the corral
will grow longer.

My *wayhel* is suffering in the mountain.
My animal soul has fallen off the hill.
She's at the end of her rope,
at the last link in the chain.
Lend me your ten toes,
your ten fingers
to guide my *wayhel* back into her tiger cave.
Back into the green cave where my spirit lives.

Lift her up with a cloth that smells of roses.
With a rose, lift me up.
Lay me down in the shade of a vine.

Elder Brother Who Feeds the Souls:
Guardian of the Corral:
Bearer of Time:
Spin around in a circle, turn in a square.
Don't let the tiger out, the jaguar out,
the wolf,
the coyote,
the fox,

the weasel.
Herd them together, don't let them go.
I've brought you turkey eggs.
I've brought pigeon stones
for the hand and the foot
of She Who Sees from Far Away Through Dreams.

Keep my animal alive for many years
with pine pitch,
tree sap,
rose water,
fir cone, laurel knot,
thirteen essences of *tilil*.

Make my days longer with the sweat of your legs,
your hands that glow green as precious jade,
your green, green blood.

Carry me, embrace me
and my tiger, and my jaguar.

This is all I will bother you with
in the name of the flowers.

Let my animal spirit live
many more years
in the pages of the Book,
in its letters, its paintings,
on the whole surface of the Earth.

   —Manwela Kokoroch

FEEDING THE BLACK DOG

Good dog:
Take your tortilla.

When I die,
you will carry me

across the water
to Where They Warm Our Bones.

Come here,
eat your tortilla.

I won't hit you.
I won't kill you.

Don't buck me off in the river, dog.
Don't leave me in the middle of the lake.

Good dog:
Eat your tortilla.
          —*Munda Tostón*

A WAKE

Great Aunt:
There's no end to sickness,
death won't go away.

At least you're not the only one;
I'm going to die too.

All of us will become Earth.
All of us will be mud.

There are no two ways about it:
I'm coming right behind you, here beside you.

Little marigold:
Flower of death:

How many are buried beneath this cross?
How many underneath our prayers?
                    —*Maruch Méndes Péres*

A DRINKING SONG BY THE WIFE OF THE ALPEREZ

Give me the pardon of five men!
For I shouted in your house, *Kajval*.

I drank liquor.
I drank *chicha*.

I rinsed out the jug.
I washed the glass of the sky.
Kajval, I spat.

Your daughter was drunk, Great Old Santiago.
I carried you in the procession.

Watched after your shadow.
Filled the cave with the echo of your song.

Tied up a bull.
Carried the *Niño Tila*.
Embraced the gods.

Sang on the Earth.
Grew in the Earth.

I saw what was grand.
I saw what was small.
                    —*Pasakwala Kómes*

DANCE OF THE PERFUMED WOMAN

God willing, María!
God willing, Luchita!

Ojalá, Maruquita!
Ojalá, Chinita!

María is dancing.
Rosario is dancing.

I am a woman, I am a woman, I am a real woman.
I am a girl, I am a girl, I am a real girl.

The women are dancing.
The girls are dancing.

Pick off, pick off your lice, women.
Comb, comb your hair, *niñas*.

I am a perfumed woman.
I am a perfumed girl.

I am a *puta* woman.
I am a *puta* girl.

The Sun is dancing.
The Moon is dancing.
   —*Tonik Nibak*

NOTES ON THE CREATORS

OVER A HUNDRED AND FIFTY PEOPLE COLLABORATED to write, illustrate, and create this book, among them singers, seers, witchwives, washer women, sugar beer brewers, conjurers, native bearers, prayer makers, soothsayers, sorceresses, dyers, diviners, hired mourners, spinners, shepherdesses, babysitters, millers, maids, bookbinders, spellbinders, cornharvesters, great-grandmothers, sharecroppers, necromancers, exorcists, coffee pickers, potters, crazy women, midwives, planters, woodlanders, bonesetters, troublemakers, spiritualists, mothers-in-law, peddlers, gravediggers, fireworks makers, drinkers, hags, beggars, bakers, basket weavers, shamanesses, liars, computers, *comagres*, sculptresses, muses, and even men. We have made this book "as we make our children," in the words of Petú Xantis, "with the strength of our flesh and the birds of our heart."

> In the land of *Som Chi*, the Eloquent Conjurer,
> In the land of *Som Chi*, Spinner of Incantations.
> —*Ritual de los Bacabes*

I first came to know the conjurers in Cotzilnab or "Rooster Lake," an hour's walk from the church of Magdalenas, a Tzotzil Mayan hamlet in Chiapas where ethnologist Chip Morris took me in 1975. I lived there for two years in the houses of three very different old women, Rosa Xulemhó, Markarita Váskes Kómes, and María Álvares Jiménes or Me' Avrila (Mrs. Avrila).

Rosa Xulemhó is a sorceress and a midwife, head of a huge Chamula clan. She herself gave birth to fifteen children, nine of whom died in infancy. She keeps sheep and supervises the planting of field cabbages, fava beans, squash, and foot-long radishes. Rosa taught me to spin wool and how to dye it with dodder and bitter herbs. Her house is filled with incense and incantations for curing. This is Rosa's blessing for a newborn:

> Boll of cotton,
> soft as silk,
> cute as a pompon,
> newly born,

planted
on the Earth
by my lord San Juan.

Markarita Váskes had been a mother and housewife all her life, and Me' Avrila, who never had children, was the ceremonial weaver and Keeper of the Traditions of Magdalenas. Together we recorded and wrote down the stories of their lives. Thanks to a great deal of help from John Burstein and Alejandra Álvarez and a grant from the Pellizzi Collection, their autobiographies were published in 1978 in the bilingual book *Slo'il jchiltaktik.*

Markarita and Me' Avrila's memory went as far back as the 1902 eruption of the volcano Santa Maria—"when the ash fell." They remembered a time of famine when it did not rain and there was no corn, only green bananas and fern roots to subsist on. They knew stories from the Mexican Revolution and the time in the 1930s when soldiers came to burn the saints. Markarita laughed as she told how the images were hidden in the woods and how the religious officials fooled the soldiers by lighting a bonfire outside the church and saying, "Not to worry, see, we have already burned our saints."

Me' Avrila knew stories about other historical events such as the War of Saint Rose in 1869. Her vocabulary was old fashioned and now and again she surprised me with a phrase out of the *Popol Vuh*, such as *"Likan ak', likan te'"* (Rise up vine, rise up tree).

The autobiographies were illustrated with couplets recited on the Day of the Dead and other fiestas, and prayers in verse for learning to weave, for marriage, and religious *cargos*. Markarita Váskes shared with me the poetic speech she made when she received for safekeeping the sacred coffer containing the Virgin's necklace:

Stand behind us
when we are sitting,
when we are squatting
in this dump,
my dirty house.
Can you stand it?

Hope it's not too much
for you to put up with
my filth,
my garbage,
Kajval, Holy Mother.

When I presented Markarita and Me' Avrila with the first copies of their book, Markarita rewarded me with a turkey leg and Me' Avrila said, "Now I can die, because everything has been said and written down." Both of them are dead now.

Tonik Nibak of Zinacantán was also a grand woman who had a great way with words. Robert M. Laughlin remembers her as the best storyteller he has ever known. Tonik worked as a servant in San Cristóbal from the time she was seven, then became a weaver, but she dedicated her last years to making life impossible for her sons-in-law and to selling roses from door to door in San Cristóbal. Tonik would knock on my door at six in the morning and I could never resist buying her load of Castile roses. Together we translated into Spanish the narrations of Me' Avrila and Markarita; every day we worked until the shadow of the house touched a certain rock in the patio. Tonik would secretly move the rock when she was in a hurry to go. Now she is gone forever.

A day's walk over the mountain from Me' Avrila's house is the village of Chenalhó, where María Xila or Me' Komate (Mrs. Komate) lived with her husband Mol Komate (Old Man Komate), the Master of Music and Ritual Advisor of San Pegro. Mol Komate was a sage, what the Japanese call a living treasure. Because her old man flirted with me, María Xila laughingly referred to me as *jk'exol*, "my replacement," but her old man died before she did.

Like a poor relation, I moved from one family to another, house to house, village to village. I was shocked by the living conditions in the eroded highlands of the poorest state of Mexico. Father, mother, aunts, a grandmother or two, numerous children including a few adopted orphans share the one-room Tzotzil house with dogs, pigs, lambs, and turkeys. Apart from some clay pots and gourds, a bucket, a griddle and a grinding stone, perhaps a battery-operated radio kept in a clear plastic bag, a machete, and a spoon, there isn't much to see inside the dark, windowless space. Only three sacred hearthstones in the middle of the dirt floor, a plume of smoke, an old woman kneeling before a tiny altar in the corner. She ties pine branches to a cross, lights a row of candles, blows on coals, drops *copal* in a brazier, chanting in a low voice:

Flowery Woman,
Mother in Flower:
Come with me on the way up.
Stay beside me on the way down.
—*Maruch Péres Méndes*

The Tzotzils carry huge burdens on tumplines, they plant their corn on steep, rocky slopes, weave clothes on backstrap looms, grind corn by hand and pat out mountains of tortillas over smoky fires. Despite the hard work, the extreme cold, the vermin, the mud, the lack of water, the hunger, the total absence of what I call comfort, such poor people constantly surround themselves with poetry of their own making. In my culture, poetry is considered a luxury. Among the Tzotzils it is an essential part of daily life.

The art of speaking well is very important for the Maya. Knowing many ritual couplets is an accomplishment that inspires great respect. The beauty of the women's incantations haunted me, their images, rhythms, metaphors. I began to tape-record the chants in my attempt to understand them. I could find no books about Mayan women's poetry, although *Perils of the Soul* by Calixta Guiteras Holmes greatly helped my understanding of the traditional metaphors, ritual vocabulary, *wayhels*, and birds of the heart. I learned a great deal too, from Gary Gossen's *Chamulas in the World of the Sun*, the novels of Rosario Castellanos, Carter Wilson's *Crazy February* and *A Green Tree and A Dry Tree*, and of course from Robert M. Laughlin's shelf of magical publications.

It wasn't easy to be accepted by Tzotzil people. Only after months of living together, when I came down with acute appendicitis, did my hosts begin to consider me a human being. They said they were afraid if I died the army would come, so they cured me with herbs and prayers. After that, people seemed to realize I was a mortal.

One of my first true friends was María Tzu, whom I met in 1975 on the top of the mountain where she lived, between Magdalenas and Chenalhó. One night as I lay on the floor of her house watching the play of the shadows on the rafters, María Tzu came over, knelt beside me, and began to touch me tentatively, as though I were a wild animal she wanted to tame. She gently explored my entire body with her hands and then declared, "You are a real woman, aren't you? You could probably even have children."

María Tzu is the mother of seven and a master dyer who uses wild plants to tint hand-spun wool. She was awarded the National Folk Art Prize for her fine spinning and weaving, and a ceremonial *huipil* she created is featured in the exhibit, *The Courtly Art of the Ancient Maya*. María and her family were expelled from their land a few years ago for becoming Jehovah's Witnesses. She lives now in La Hormiga, a Mayan barrio on the outskirts of San Cristóbal, in a tiny cement house with her grown children, her sons and daughters-in-law, sixty-seven grandchildren, and three urban sheep. Everyone makes *huaraches* out of old truck tires. María Tzu contributed five incantations to this book and several paintings. Even though she claims to have cast aside her ancient Mayan customs to become a Protestant, María's born-again prayers in Tzotzil are nearly identical to those of the Fathermothers.

In the winter of 1975, practically all the children of Magdalenas died of an unidentified fever. It could have been whooping cough or swine flu. There was no clinic in the community, no western medicine, and the government authorities in San Cristóbal did not react to my pleas for help. I watched as scores of mothers buried their dead babies in the cemetery. Invariably they sang a little song to the child, giving her a last swig of Koka Kola before covering the body with earth.

> Now my carrying shawl is empty.
> I have no son, now.
>
> I am no one's mother,
> I am no one's breast.
>   —*Mikaela Moshán Culej*

Pasakwala Kómes came to Cotzilnab to cure the sick. She is a curer and witch from Santiago El Pinar, an especially impoverished town a good hour's walk from Magdalenas, where it is said *everyone* is either a thief or a witch. Pasakwala and her husband Antrés, who was also a shaman, had held the prestigious religious office of Alperes. I met them when they came to make house calls at Markarita's. Pasakwala would pulse the sick person, often *Bikit* or "Little" Pegro, the five-year-old of the family, and ask questions of his mother: Had any strangers come by on the path? Had the child fallen down? Were the neighbors envious? What had he dreamed?

Finally, Pasakwala might announce that Little Pegro's soul had gotten lost when he went with his mother to wash clothes in the river. If so, she would prescribe so many red twenty-cent candles, so many peso-striped candles, white ones and black ones of this price and the other. She always asked for incense, too, and the big orphan boy would be dispatched to buy some at the plantation owner's *tiendita* or at the store the Ladino teachers had in the one-room school. He'd always get a liter or two of *pox* and several bottles of Pexi Kola. Meanwhile, Pasakwala would plant a wooden cross in the dirt floor and dress it with sacred leaves. She spread pine needles on the floor before the cross and blew on the coals of her incense burner until they burned red enough to turn a handful of incense into a cloud of smoke.

Pasakwala's curing prayers were charged with words and names I had never heard before and could not find in the dictionaries: Hurricane Woman, Butterfly Man, Mother Breast, *Kaxil*. I was captivated by the spell of her verses. My wildest dream had been to document the life story of a Mayan shaman, and here she was—and an extraordinary witch at that. I asked Pasakwala if she would tell me the story of her life and she immediately said, "Yes." The very next day I went to her house with my tape recorder and Pasakwala told me all about how she had learned to cure. She described the book with red covers the Fathermothers held in her dream, with the spells written in gold letters. Then she said she wanted to hear what I had taped. I was dying to hear it too, but much to my consternation the recorder had not registered one word. Pasakwala laughed at me. Nevertheless, she was willing to tell her story a second time.

I put new batteries into the apparatus and Pasakwala began again. The second telling was even better. She provided details of how, as a little girl, she had played at curing her dolls, building tiny altars in the back yard out of wild orchids and pine needles. I was ecstatic until I rewound the tape and realized that again I hadn't recorded anything. Pasakwala was very patient with me. Wasting time seemed to amuse her. She generously agreed to repeat her story a third time.

I changed the batteries again, cleaned the heads with alcohol and put in a new cassette. Pasakwala spoke at length about Mayan witchcraft; most of what she said I couldn't understand because I was just learning Tzotzil, but I remember hearing the word *wayhel* a lot, which the dictionary said meant animal soul companion, dream, shamanism. She spoke for ninety minutes about her *cargo* as the *Alperes'* wife, reciting obscure couplets I have never heard again.

But the tape was bewitched and it didn't register anything at all. Pasakwala found my frustration hilarious. The recorder, once out of Pasakwala's house, never failed me again.

Manwela Kokoroch was an *h-ilol* and midwife from Laguna Petej, Chamula. I consider her prayer *To the Bearer of Time* to be the most beautiful text in this collection. Manwela lived to be a hundred years old.

The late Petú Xantis was a witch from Pantelhó. I met her one night when the moon was full and I was giving a refresher course on the lost Tzotzil tradition of natural dyes. As the teacher, I was terribly embarrassed if the colors didn't turn out right, and that night everything went wrong. "It's because some woman is menstruating," said one student. "Don't be superstitious," another scolded, "the truth is that one of us is pregnant." At that moment, Petú looked in through the street door and shouted to me, "Any fool knows you can't dye when the moon is full." I convinced her to take me on as an apprentice.

I ran into María Kartones in 1975 in San Cristóbal. She was a mad woman who shouted in the street, heaving stones at doors, running away from pursuers that only she could see. María would tarry at every puddle in the cobbled pavement, smearing her face and hair with mud. After years of this, she seemed to be wearing a mask and a clay helmet.

According to Tzotzil mythology, the Mud Heads, dwarf mule drivers in the Underworld, daub themselves with clay as protection from the heat of the Sun. When they are able to balance a load on the back of a rabbit, according to the story, the Mud Heads will come up to the surface of the Earth and we will go to live down below.

When the European armies first brought Christ to these lands, the women put mud on their faces to make themselves ugly and undesirable to their violators. María Kartones is said to have been raped by soldiers as a young girl. She now lives near Mexico City in the San Bernardino asylum. Her portrait can be found on every postcard rack in San Cristóbal. Antonio Turok photographed her in 1976, the same day I was able to record her screaming:

> Protect me from the soldiers.
> They are killing me, *AAAAAAY!*
>
> I don't want to cover myself in Earth.
> I don't want to dress myself in mud.

Loxa Jiménes Lópes, weaver and seer from Epal Ch'en, "Many Caves," Chamula, is a singer and painter with a number of texts and paintings in this book. She also worked forming the masks for the cover of the hand-made edition of this book. Loxa's twelve-year-old granddaughter Laura Pale painted a page to honor the dead.

Loxa's daughter Xpetra Ernándes Jiménes is a member of the council of coordinators of the Leñateros Workshop in San Cristóbal, where the original *Incantations by Mayan Women* was created and published. Xpetra collaborated in the translation of the spells into Spanish and English and also contributed several of her own. Over the course of the years, Xpetra sought out and encouraged many painters and seers, made masks, and dyed the endpapers black.

Xunka' Unka' Utz'Utz' Ni' produces fireworks in Chamula. She grows bamboo to form the structure for the exploding "castles" and "bulls" that are set off in the celebrations; she mixes gunpowder, braids fuses, and with the leftover canes, Xunka' weaves baskets.

Mikaela Días Días, a weaver from San Andrés (Sacam Ch'en de los Pobres), keeps shop at the House of Weaving, Sna Jolobil, a cooperative in San Cristóbal. Her husband accused her of having "red hands" that kept her from giving him a son. He took a second wife who was also unable to have children. The three of them lived together under the same roof for just about forever. As the Tzotzils say: "Eternity is very long, especially towards the end." Finally the man died. Mikaela is one of the important painters of this book. She died just as the book went to press.

Luisa Hernándes, nicknamed Sluz, the Virgin Weaver for the Moon of Tenejapa, is another key artist. She used to work in a Cantonese restaurant in San Cristóbal; now she teaches back-strap weaving and always seems to wear a big smile.

Verónika Taki Vaj, a seven-year-old-girl from Chalchihuitán, sings the *Song of the Little Deer*. Way out in the sticks where she lives, most of the men are hunters and their game bags are sewn from raccoon skins. Veronika has a little purse that her uncle made her out of a deer's foot with a tiny hood on it. It's for keeping bits of fool's gold for hunting tigers. Veronika's song is about the deer who carries the Earth Lord on its back to Guatemala to get gunpowder for his lightning bolts. There are Mayan peddlers who bring "Deer Brand" firewater and "Tiger Brand" firecrackers from Guatemala to sell at the Tzotzil fiestas.

María Patixtán Likán Chitom is a woman of tremendous energy and artistic spirit. She cuts a powerful figure in her handwoven black *huipil* adorned with brightly colored pompons and splendid Venetian glass necklaces. María creates human figures out of wood, clay, rags, corn-husks, thatch. Had she been born in Europe or Mexico City instead of Setelton, Chamula, María Patixtán would most likely be as famous as Frida Kalho. Her house is filled with musicians who play the harp day and night; full of flowers and contentment; women making tortillas amid the smoke of incense, people drinking and singing as is the custom when a woman has the *cargo* of *Martoma Sakramento*.

> I am woman, the women,
> I am girl, the girl.
>
> The Flowering Mother of the Sky,
> the Flowering Mother of Happiness.
>
> I am the woman *Martoma,*
> I am the *Martoma* woman.
> I am the *Martoma* Nina,
> I am the *Martoma* Nina of San Juan.
> —*María Patixtán Likan Chitóm*

She and eleven other women are the Midwives of the Sun. They attend his birth on Christmas Eve, easing his journey toward the light with song.

> Baby *Emmanuel,*
> Tiny *Xalik,*
> Little Traveler from Far Away,
> Little Godfather,
> Baby *Kajval.*

During a recording session in the fall of 1999, María Patixtán Likan Chitóm described how as a little girl she would sing to her sheep in the pastures of Chamula. I felt a rush of excitement as I listened to this children's song and then, much to my astonishment, María went on to sing another, a monologue directed to the Moon Goddess as sung by a little girl who is learning to weave.

Ay, Mother Moon,
Ay, Sacred Godmother,
Woman in Flower,
Girl in Flower,
la la ti la laaa.
My little loom is all tangled up.

Now it's fixed,
my little loom,
my little skirt is finished,
my blouse is woven, *Kajval.*
My skirt is so beautiful!

In January of 2000, Roco of the rock band *La Maldita Vecindad y los Hijos del Quinto Patio* and I visited María Patixtán Likan Chitóm's ceremonial house in Chamula center, and were fortunate enough to witness (and record) María teaching her two tiny granddaughters, Marta and Petrona Patixtán Patixtán, to sing the song entitled *Bolom Chon*:

María: Learn the step, *Bolom Chon.*
Your paws are so long.

Girls: Long paws, *Bolom Chon.*

María: Tiger who dances in the sky.

Girls: Tiger who dances in the sky.

María: Tiger who dances on the Earth.

Girls: Tiger who dances on the Earth.

María: Your beard is long, Dancing Tiger.

Girls: *Your beard is long, Dancing Tiger.*

María: *Yellow Sheep in the sky.*

Girls: *Yellow Sheep in the sky.*

María: *Yellow Sheep on the Earth.*

Girls: *Yellow Sheep on the Earth.*

When we asked María Patixtán to paint for this book, she said she had no time and brought her eight-year-old grandson Marselino Patixtán to paint in her stead. Marselino is now twelve and is studying to be a shaman, specializing in the terminally ill. He is learning to guide the dying across the threshold between life and death, negotiating the border crossing through immigration and customs. Marselino's mother Jasinta Lópes Lópes painted *The Face of the Sun in Eclipse*.

Estela Hernández Téllez has eleven brothers and she suckled her little Mauricio as she painted and repainted *The Mothers of Corn*.

Manwela Kómes Kómes of Huixtan and Rosa Lópes Kómes from Oxchuc pick coffee beans; they are also learning to read and write at Fortaleza de la Mujer Maya (FOMMA)—"Strength of the Maya Women"—founded by writers Petrona de la Cruz Cruz and Isabel Juárez Espinosa. Manwela and Rosa came to the Woodlanders' Workshop to paint, carrying babies in their shawls. Rosa also brought her newborn child in her arms and her big girl, who is two, hanging onto her skirt. I was very much taken by the force of Rosa's painting style, so much so that I sought her out in the coffee plantation to ask her about her life. She told me that two days before she had painted the *Xpakinté* (on page 42) she had buried her husband, murdered by a man who mistook him for someone else.

The *rezandera* or "prayer sayer" Munda Tostón has a little stand in the market of San Cristóbal where she sells ski masks to the Zapatistas.

Shepherdess Maruch Méndes Péres is the author of *Songs of the Drunken Woman*. Maruch is not much of a drinker, however, and claims she never married because she can't stand drunks.

She lives in Catixtik, Chamula with two little girls she adopted, Xvel and Marta Méndes. Now it seems that Maruch has also adopted Xvel and Marta's three siblings and also their birth mother, Dominga. All of them have changed their last names to Méndes. The *Leñateros* were trying to get in touch with Maruch last year to pay her royalties from the sales of the Spanish version of this book, but were told that she had died, and would be buried that very day. All of us from the Workshop piled into a hired van packed full of flowers and we headed off sadly to Maruch's hamlet. There were hundreds of people in mourning outside of her house, including Maruch herself, who was so overjoyed to witness our arrival at the funeral that she forgot for a moment her sadness over the death of her elder sister—also named Maruch Méndes.

Antel Péres Ok'il is a Chamula potter who creates the enormous urns used for the fermented gruel served on the Day of the Dead.

Petra Tzonte' Vitz lives on the highest and most sacred mountain top of the Chiapas Highlands: Tzontevitz. She and her husband are the keepers of the cave where San Juan lives. Both are shamans, but due to hard times, he has become an illegal immigrant and works at a slaughter house in Tennessee.

Petra Bakbolom is a conjurer from Chamula who specializes in spells for children who have lost their souls. Her husband distills *pox*, moonshine rum.

Rominka Vet is from *Ya'al Mut*, "Bird Water," Chamula. Her family produces charcoal for the kitchens and chapels of San Cristóbal. She and her mother and grandmother go out of their house at dawn carrying bundles of charcoal on tumplines. They walk for miles through the fog to where they set up shop on the sidewalk near the Guadalupe church selling coals for braziers and incense burners.

Jwana Te La Krus Posol carries her baby in a sling on her back as she sells friendship bracelets to tourists in downtown San Cristóbal. Her husband is in jail for attempting to hold up a *Pexi Kola* truck.

Roxa Hernándes Díaz is the master weaver for the Virgin of the Rosary of San Andrés Larrainzar, where the San Andrés Accords were signed by the Zapatistas and representatives of the government of Mexico. Roxa is coauthor of a little book about natural dyes called *Bon*, and founder of the Weaving House, Sna Jolobil, the cooperative school for weavers and dyers in San Andrés. Roxa is the mother of seven children, grandmother of many, and my godmother. Her beautiful portrait can be seen on the covers of anthropology books and on postcards sent all over the world, but Roxa, daughter of a shaman, lives in the same extreme poverty in which she was born. She told us this story of the Naked Woman:

A woman went out of her house. She bolted her door and headed for the woods. "I can't stand to live with men anymore," she said, and she went to sleep alone in the forest. By night she watched the constellations. Her only fire was in the sky where the Moon heats up her cooking pot among the stars of Orion. With the passing of the years, the poor woman's clothes wore out. She was naked when she died and the jaguar buried her. The only clue they found were these couplets scribbled on a scrap of dark paper:

Three stones in the sky
glow among the stars.

Three sisters bake their tortillas
in the coals of the Milky Way.
—*Roxa Hernández Díaz*

OVER THE THIRTY YEARS it has taken to create this book made by Mayan hands, hundreds of incantations were taped in dozens of Tzotzil hamlets. The transcription of the tapes fill thousands of pages. Faced with the impossibility of translating and publishing every word, we were obliged to choose only the most outstanding texts to be included. The fragments of songs that illustrate the essays are for the most part bits of spells that could not fit into the anthology.

Eighty women, all insisting that they didn't know how to paint, painted for three years, consuming lakes full of India ink and mountains of paper, to produce the graphics that accompany the texts. Many more paintings were produced than we could reproduce.

The Tzotzil writer and used clothes seller who for more than a quarter century has worked on this book, flirting with the seers, transcribing the tapes in Tzotzil, translating and correcting the different versions, and who appears in the credits as Father of the Book, who finally for the U.S. English edition of this book is willing to be named as Xalik Guzmán Bakbolom instead of his alias Xun Okotz, wrote me the following letter:

OK, Ámbar:

Look, I want to tell you something about what you said to me on the Monday, the eleventh of March: I am going to scold you a little. But just a bit, truly: I don't want you to put my name in your book, because it's not just my work; there is Xpetra's work, Xpetra's mother's work, the work of María Tzu, of Xunka' Utz'utz' Ni'. I'd feel guilty about taking all the credit, and anyway the texts are really awful; practically like witchcraft. It was very ugly what you read to me that time: "That a gigantic termite eat his penis, that a snake bite his belly, that a wasp sting his asshole, that a worm devour his heart," you said. So when you told me you were going to put me down as co-translator, well, son of a bitch! I got scared, because if my Chamula friends see my name in the book, they are going to kill me. They are going to say that I am a witch: they are going to ask, "Why did you say that, you bastard?" And so, please Ámbar, don't put my name in the book. Say that Maryan Péres Tzu or Juan Kómes Okotz did it, that would be good; no problem, but otherwise I am going to die before my time, and what a shame that my house will be only half built when I die! My Chamula friends have ugly thoughts, and so I ask you as a special favor not to use my real name. But anyhow, I don't want you to think I am scolding you. I still want to work on our book, if you want me to. Let me know if you can read my writing, if my words speak to you, if you can hear what I'm saying. Be careful, Ámbar, that the *Xpakinté* doesn't take you off to its cave; because the *Xpakinté* is not sure if you have a husband or not.
   —Xun

The flavor of Xalik Guzmán Bakbolom's and Xpetra Ernándes's speech enriched the translations of the Tzotzil texts enormously. The bilingual Mayas in Chiapas speak a dialect of Spanish known as *castía*, which conserves many forms of sixteenth-century Spanish, as a bit of amber holds the wings of time.

The German tongue is considered appropriate for training horses, Italian for courting women, French for diplomats, Spanish is said to be for addressing God. Without a doubt, Tzotzil Maya is a language suited to magic.

For his assistance in the deciphering of the spells, I am eternally grateful to a poet who passes as an anthropologist; a Zinacantec Maya who disguised himself as a gringo at birth and—using the pseudonym Robert M. Laughlin—created, among other notable books, *The Great Tzotzil Dictionary of San Lorenzo Zinacantán*. To give readers a taste, we reproduce here an entry from this wonderwork containing thirty thousand Tzotzil Maya words:

metz'ta, tv. incapacitate, prevent, cast evil eye, sanitize, protect, cure or empower by magic. To incapacitate a devil or a snake, tobacco or garlic is thrown at it. When corn is stolen from a field, the owner may make a cross of the corn stalks that have been stripped of ears and stand it in the center or in a corner of the field so that Our Lord will punish the robber with poverty and death. The same effect may be produced by drawing a cross on the footprints of the robber. To prevent the flesh of a charcoal-cruncher or *yalem bek'et* from re-adhering, salt is rubbed on it. To prevent a weasel that has crossed one's path from shortening one's life, and to ensure that it will die in its den, three crosses are made on the path with one's foot. To cause hail to stop falling, three pans of embers, three loom bars and three bodkins are flung at the hail. To ensure that a jaguar will not toss back one's bullets, a person sleeping in the woods will wrap the wad with three pubic hairs and three hairs from his arm pit and insert it in the rifle barrel, or he will break wind on the rifle. To make an enemy's field of corn die, a person sprinkles tobacco on it. To make an enemy's peach tree die, a stick of pine is buried at its foot. If the wife of the owner of an avocado tree is pregnant, she must take three bites out of three avocadoes lest the fruit be spoiled. When a religious official or groom has a bull slaughtered, their assistants bite the raw meat three times lest it be contaminated by the pregnancy of the wife or mistress of one of the party. To tame a mean mule, its neck is rubbed three times with a broom. To rid a corn field of raccoon, a naked boy and a naked girl walk around the edge of the field three times or an adult scatters garlic and tobacco around the edge. Opossums and raccoons reportedly can be prevented from entering the corn field by preparing a bed of straw for them six inches long placed on each side of the field. Raccoons may also be discouraged from entering the corn field if the farmer constructs a platform in the trees at the edge of the field, lies down on it, and calls out to the raccoons, "Let's sleep together." To rid a corn field of June bug grubs, a man may take a greasy, old skirt of an old woman and, holding it aloft like a flag, walk around the field three times. Alternatively, he may take two grubs and place them head to head, or one across the other, and bury them in one of their tunnels in that position. To prevent wind damage, a tip of the palm fronds distributed on St. Peter Martyr Day is tied to the corn plants at the four corners of the field. To protect a corn field in high wind, the owner will call out, *"Tzotzan me kunen chob mu me xalomik un"* / "Be strong my little corn fields, please do not fall down / so that the 'wind' will leave." To cure a mule of "wind," its belly is struck three times with a woman's sash, its tail is cropped in a cruciform design and a copper coin is passed over the tail. To cure a person of yellow spot on his eye, thirteen black beans, variously three or thirteen silver five-cent pieces together with white salt are placed outside over night to let the dew fall upon them. They are applied to the eye to reduce the "heat." *Poslom* is cured by rinsing one's leg with a woman's urine, rubbing it with tobacco and garlic and then binding it with a piece of an old skirt. To ensure that a rifle fires well, thirteen chilis are put in the barrel which is then held over the fire until the chilis are roasted.

I was very much inspired by the prose style of Robert M. Laughlin's books, especially the fascinating introductions he wrote for his collections of Tzotzil words, dreams, stories, prayers, diaries and historic documents. Laughlin's writing is enriched with gossip, jokes, woodlore and myth; the result is pure poetry.

My godfather Guadalupe Domínguez from Tierra Blanca, Zinacantán, introduced me to the art of telling stories, a style he learned from his Fathermothers.

Calixta Guiteras Holmes, whom I never had the pleasure of meeting, cleared up a number of my doubts in her beautiful book, *Perils of the Soul*. William Holland's *Medicina maya en los altos de Chiapas* was also very useful, and I was especially inspired by the language of *Ch'ulel: una etnografía de las almas tzeltales*, the work of Pedro Pitarch. Dr. Pitarch's poetic prose concerning the bird of the heart and its flight among the naguals of Cancuc bewitched me and influenced my translation of the hexes of Munda Tostón and others. An example from Pitarch:

Where we desire the caress of the word
where we desire the word,
it comes by itself
to the center of the belly,
to the center of the chest.
How much will his heart bear now?
How much will his word hear now?
You won't find the word, you will say,
you won't get to the word, you will say,
I found it singing, you will say,
I found it whistling, you will say,
it came as a book, you will say,
I got here first, you will say.

From our first meeting in 1978, Juan Bañuelos encouraged my efforts to collect and translate Mayan poetic texts. Maestro Juan proofread the Spanish version of this book.

Jacinto Arias, a writer trained in anthropology at Princeton and a native of San Pedro Chenalhó, corrected the Tzotzil along with his nephew, writer Enrique Pérez López. As founders of CELALI, the Organization of Amerindian Writers, these passionate crusaders for the creation and publication of books in Native American languages inspired our work through their examples.

The Canadian poet and artist Carol Karasik edited the texts of the Spanish edition, greatly contributing to its coherence. In addition to writing the grant proposals that made it possible to produce the book in Spanish, Carol typed the texts over a thousand and one times in Tzotzil, and was midwife and accomplice in everything. She weeded, pruned, grafted, and transplanted the sprouts so the garden would come to flower. Her good taste is reflected in the plastic aspects of the book itself and the beauty of the texts.

The knowledge and vast experience of editor and proofreader Humberto Pérez Matus also contributed enormously to the editions in both Spanish and English. It is Mademoiselle Espejo, however, who always has the last word in everything. Ena, a twenty-year-old cat, spent years purring on my lap during retyping and revising.

My dear friend Carter Wilson, who learned Tzotzil when he lived in Chamula in the 1960s, and who has written several novels since then, claims to be the "copy editor" of the English texts, although I believe the correct term to describe his contribution would include the roles of muse and god. Carter, Tonik Nibak's *compagre*, has been the calm voice on the emergency radio, talking me in for my first landing. Here are some examples from e-mail:

Ámbar: Carter, do you think the animal souls that have been captured by the *Pujuk* are held captives chained or tied with ropes awaiting sacrifice in the way that prisoners of war were held by the Ancient Maya as shown in the murals of Bonampak?

Carter: You ask your questions and suddenly it's EXACTLY 39 years ago and a rainy night in Navenchauk and I'm out in the rain (holding something, either an incense pot or a chicken or something) with the *h-ilol* and it's 3 a.m. in the morning and we are WHOA! really wasted, and thunder and lightning all around that valley and the *h-ilol* is down on his knees pounding the earth and begging / cajoling for the return of the missing parts from the soul corral of this youngish woman (herself warm in bed, having already, I think, had her bath in bayleaf water, and actually pretty much recovered from whatever was wrong with her physically) and my STRONGEST sensation is of how demanding the curer is (should he be so forthright?), but also at some level so INTIMATE with the controlling forces, talking with them, begging them. And how do I remember it's July 3, 1964? Later that night, I drive the entire curing group up into San Cris and then up to Zinacantán and we start climbing mountains.

About noon the next day we're eating cold chicken and tortillas and hardboiled eggs when the noon bells ring down in the valley and I think, "Hmm, 4th of July picnic in Zinacantán." I would imagine yes, that's how the bodies are bound. Those statues, the stucco ones without heads, at Toniná are in the same positions (seated, hands tied behind backs, necks turned in odd positions) as the figures at Bonampak. —XX, Carter

Dear Carter: OK! I got the whole book patted together today. Nineteen new incantations...which you can weed out if you think they repeat or are not on the same level poetically as the others. They are still rough. There may be more. Things trickle in and then one day Doña Antonia comes over and starts reciting an hour of texts we've never heard before with new metaphors from *Chilil*—"For the Blue Jay," "To Ask Permission to Fell a Tree," "To Teach the Dumb to Speak." The transcription inspires Xpetra into dictating a couple more pieces—one "For Planting a Tree." She says you bury 3 grains of corn in the hole for the little tree and then you pray it not fall on you when it grows tall and you beg it to accept this corn as payment for the good the tree will do for you. You thank the tree for being there.

> For tying the loom onto,
> so I can weave in the shade,
> for the chickens to roost in,
> and so the birds can sleep.

And another from Xpetra to *Kaxail*, asking permission to use her body, her clay to daub and plaster the new house,

> Otherwise the *Pukuj* will eat me,
> the Woman of the Woods will scare me,
> the Monster with its Feet on Backwards will come,
> the Boogey Man with a Hat Like a Griddle,
> the Charcoal Cruncher, the Mat Stripper,
> the snake, the jaguar, the coyote, the fox, the owl,
> the night hummingbird, the bat.
> *Kaxail*, Holy Breast, Sacred Wildwood.

Anyway, now I'm finishing a simulacrum of a Table of Contents and a Credits/ Legal page. Still working on the Tzotzil corrections, but now TODAY, I'm going to go through the WHOLE thing, try to clean out the dirt from under its fingernails, attempt to cure the soul of that last part. (*You may have to take its heart out, Carter. I offer it to you in exchange for my sanity.*) —XX, A.

Year after year during "crazy February," Carter and I attend Carnival in Chenalhó. We hang out with María Xila and Mol Komate's son Bernancio who has taken over the ceremonial duties of his late father and plays the drum in all the processions day and night. We are friends with the ritual transvestites of the fiesta, the *Me'el* and the *Me' Ka'benal* (aforementioned sex-education teachers and ritual curers). We especially enjoy drinking a little *chicha* in the early morning while the *J-ik'aletik* darken their faces with soot from the base of a griddle. We always watch as the Kruz Pat, "wild boys" who form part of the entourage, bedizen their bodies with lime and red annatto, using the mouth of a *Pexi Kola* bottle to print circles on their chests and backs.

Writer Miriam Wolfe Laughlin is a close friend who has seen the magic of the Maya first-hand. Mimi learned the hard life of a Tzotzil woman through years of living in Zinacantán where she did her family's washing in the creek. Mimi was kind enough to read over the manuscript of this book and share with us her comments and criticism.

John Burstein, Maríclaire Acosta and Marcey Jacobson also read and commented on the manuscript before it went to press.

Juan Antonio Ascencio and Elena Poniatowska prayed.

Railboomer Linda Niemann sent the Chattanooga choo choo down to Chiapas to get this show on the road.

Giovanni Proiettis and Maribel Rotondo gave us food for thought over delicious suppers.

Tila Rodriguez-Past helped with everything.

—Ámbar Past

NOTES

on *Incantations by Mayan Women*
A hand-made, hand-typeset and hand-printed edition produced in San Cristóbal, Chiapas in 2005.
This beautiful book is available through the Taller Leñateros at www.tallerlenateros.com.

Incantations by Mayan Women is the collective work of Taller Leñateros, the "Woodlanders' Workshop," a cultural society of Maya and mestizo women and men who produce something in between a performance piece and an act of witchcraft. Over wood fires in the patio boil huge kettles of corn husks, gladiola stems, heart of maguey, palm leaves, recycled women's cotton *huipil* blouses, banana trunks, rattan, lichen, banana leaves, bridal veil fern, *mahagua*, beanpods, maguey tongues, reeds, coconut shells, grass, papyrus, cattails, pampas grass and bamboo, along with recycled paper and who knows what other raw material for papermaking. There are baskets full of papyrus, liana vines, lichen, and moss; the stuff of dreams is nearly always something "useless." We beat the fibers in a mill which spins by bicycle power. We spread the paper in the Sun, and while it dries we print poems on oak leaves and pansy petals. Conjure-women sing at the foot of the avocado tree. Loxa Jiménes Lópes, Xunka' Utz' Utz' Ni, and María Tzu paint amid the odor of the honeysuckle. Our silkscreen alchemists work from Sun to Sun, from Moon to Moon, transforming natural light into bougainvillea-color images. We cut, fold, sew, glue, bind, and wrap. The workshop produces a literary magazine, a rustic codex know as *La jícara*, "The Gourd," which includes translations from Native languages, testimonies, foreigners' journals, block prints, petroglyphs, and odd stuff.

Gitte Daehlin is a Norwegian artist who has been visiting Chiapas for over twenty years. She carves trees, kneads fiber paper with sawdust and cactus juice to create saints that lie in the museums of Europe. Her daughter Maritea belongs to the royal family of Cameroon. Gitte is the Creator and Maker of the mask on the cover of the original handmade version of *Incantations*.

Initially I imagined the front of the book to be an altar with candles and sacred pine needles somehow attached, but one afternoon I dreamed this face of the Earth. She spoke to me in my dream and told me she was the cover of the book. I found the spitting image of her face hanging on the wall in Monica and José Angel Rodríguez's house: a carved mask from a Mayan village in Guatemala which Daehlin sculpted in beeswax to create the mother mold for casting the book covers.

Starting in 1996, painter Roselia Montoya from Huixtán directed the making of the 3,333 masks for the cover of the book, using old cardboard boxes, corn silk, rabbit skin glue, tar, camphor leaves, and instant coffee. She was assisted by Xpetra Ernándes; Juan Nabor Ernándes, grandson of Loxa Jiménes Lópes; Adolfo Moshán; Julio Álvarez; María Tzu; Lucio Jiménez; Romeo Rodríguez; Cristóbal Vázquez Moshán; Pedro Álvarez; and me. When the rains came and the papers wouldn't dry, my comadre Roselia found Sun in hot country, loaded up a ten-ton truck to relocate the papermaking department in Motozintla six hours south of San Crostóbal. There she worked with José Luis Hernández, Nicolás de Paz, Simona Orozco, Gema Tamayo and the compadres Eusebio Chin Tot, Cristobalina Morales, Alex Camposeco, Juana Montejo, Elvira Tul, Rosauro Díaz Zunún, Celia Bartolón, and Andrés Andrés Andrés (his daddy's last name and his mama's last name are the same as his first name). They made 6,666 endpapers for the book and then trucked the whole shebang back up to San Cristóbal again. Xpetra Ernándes dyed the endpapers black with mud and campeachy wood and then she pressed each one smooth with her charcoal iron.

Antún Ton (Tesh Tontik) came from the other side of the sea to cut the masks one by one and open the eyes of the face of the book with a wrought-iron tool Alonso Méndez dreamed up at Moises Morales' place in the Pan Chan of Palenque. Lucio Jiménez from up on Huitepec Mountain opened a lot of eyes too.

When it came time to do the typesetting, my *compadre* Pedro Álvarez Moshán from Chilil, who for twelve years printed and distributed the famous San Cristóbal newspaper *El Tiempo*, convinced me of the necessity of buying a computer. He taught me how to use it and that's when Pasakwala Kómes, the shaman from Santiago el Pinar, came back to torture me. I have no idea how she crawled out of the bewitched tape recorder, but she got into the computer while I was typing up this text. When I got to page 262 where I complain about her pranks, the paragraphs rebelled; Pasakwala ground the words to powder. She dug her teeth into the pages and ripped off their faces. When the griddles and pots rebelled in the *Popol Vuh*, they attacked and ran after the men and women of the First Creation, they tried to:

> climb up on the houses and the houses fell down and threw them on the ground;
> they wanted to climb up the trees and the trees threw them far away; they wanted
> to enter into the caves and caves closed before them.

I know just how the people felt. I challenged Pasakwala's force and that was my ruin. We had to call in Loxa Jiménes to cleanse the computer. Loxa lit black candles, red candles, green and yellow candles, and she rubbed the screen with a black hen while praying:

> They have thrown
> the heart of the paper,
> the heart of the letters
> of the Komputer, *Kajval*,
> into the tiger's cave,
> onto the jaguar's hill.

In the spring of 2002, Loxa, Xpetra, María Tzu, Maruch Méndes, Xvel and others members of our workshop attended a fiesta in Magdalenas. Andrew Mutter, Tesh Tontik, and his legendary dog Gringo and I were drinking a soda pop in a stall when a man appeared asking if I were "Ambra." He presented himself as Bikit Pegro, my Tzotzil teacher from thirty years ago! The last time I saw him he was a four year old running after the horse that turned Markarita's sugar cane mill. Pegro invited us to the old house where I had lived with his family in 1975, where his aunt Apolonia taught me to weave in the shadow of a mango tree. Due to a fall she suffered as a little girl, Apolonia has a hunchback and walks with some difficulty. She never married and lives humbly as the poor aunt who takes care of the children in the house like a servant. Now she and Bikit Pegro are Zapatistas; they laugh when I call her *Comandanta* Apolonia.

Bikit Pegro showed us the path through the coffee plantation on the hill, up to the house of Pasakwala Kómes, the godmother and author of the disgrace of our electronic apparatus. We found the witch at home; she acted as though she didn't remember me. I explained that I had come to pay her royalties for a book. I handed over the money and took photos of her in front of her house along with her daughter and her grandchildren. As you might have guessed, the entire roll of film turned out blank.

Similarly, as I was finishing the typesetting for this book, just as I typed Pasakwala's name, my computer crashed and I lost this entire manuscript. While printing Pasakwala's name on one of the later pages in the book, our offset machine, Amada, "bit" Lucio Jimenez's finger bad enough to require four stitches. Shaman Loxa Jiménes showed up the next day and I asked her what to do. "I will burn candles for the machine next week," she offered, but I was impatient and wanted it "right now."

"But it just ate," insisted Loxa. "The machine won't get hungry again for a week or so."

When it was time, Loxa burned purple, black, yellow, pineapple colored, blue, red, green, gold and striped candles and *copal* incense. She turned our printshop into a chapel and Amada was the altar. Since Amada is red, a live red rooster was rubbed all over her rollers and gears in ritual cleaning. The bird was offered to the machine as food so that it would not be hungery for the blood of Lucio Jiménes and Daniel López Setjol as they printed this book.

The English version includes many new texts for an ever-growing collection of magic spells and drinking songs. Sound engineer Sergio San Miguel of Magic Universe was able to rescue badly deteriorated recordings made in 1975 so we could hear once more the voices of Markarita and *Me´*Avrila. He even managed to find a few couplets on the cassettes bewitched by Pasakwla Kómes.

Legendary Mayan silkscreen artist Cristóbal Vázquez Mosháan printed almost all of the silk screen graphics in the book together with Romeo Rodríguez, but the work was finished by students Lucio Jiménez, Marianao te la Kruz Tzu, youngest son of Maria Tzu, Daniel López, Julio Álvarez Moshán, and Jeremias Setjol. During months and years they have invoked the Mothers of the Night and of the Light to stamp in Solar and Lunar silk screen the original ink paintings that accompany the texts.

Antonia Moshán Culej, Xpetra Ernández, Eliza López Gómez, Petrona Ruiz Cruz, and María Tzu sewed the pages together with thread and needle so the book could be born. Antonia Moshán is the coordinator of Taller Leñateros. She is from Chilil, Huixtán, and knows candlemaking, papermaking and spicy stories.

—*Ámbar Past*

BIBLIOGRAPHY

Aguirre Beltrán, Gonzalo, *Medicina y Magia*. Mexico: Instituto Nacional Indigenista, 1963.

Ak'abal, Humberto, *Guardián de la caída de agua*. Guatemala, 1994.

Alejos, García José, *Wajalix ba t'an*, Universidad Nacional Autónoma de Mexico, 1988.

Anales de los xahil. Traducción y notas de Georges Raynaud, Miguel Angel Asturias y J.M. González de Mendoza. Mexico: Universidad Nacional Autónoma de Mexico, 1946.

Arias, Jacinto, *El mundo numinoso de los mayas: estructura y cambios contemporáneos*. Mexico: Sepsetentas 188, 1991.

Arias, Jacinto, *Ojoroxtotil (Dios Padre Providente)*, Folleto #18. Dirección de Fortalecimiento y Fomento a las Culturaas Sub-secretaría de Asuntos Indígenas del Gobierno del Estado de Chiapas, 1984.

Arias, Jacinto, *San Pedro Chenalhó: Algo de su historia, cuentos y costumbres*. Gobierno del Estado de Chiapas, Consejo Estatal de Fomento a la Investigacion y Difusion de la Cultura, Instituto Chiapaneco de Cultura, 2nd edition, 1990.

Arias, Jacinto, *Ya'yejal kolonya choro ta che'nelo; Chiapas, Historia de la Colonia de "Los Chorros" Chenalhó, Chiapas*. Gobierno del Estado de Chiapas, 1987.

Arzápalo Marín, Ramón, *El ritual de los Bacabes, con transcripción rítmica, traducción, notas, índice, glosario y cómputos estadísticas*. Mexico: Frentes para el Estudio de la Cultura Maya 5, 1987.

Barrera Vásquez, Alfredo, *Codice de Calkini, Cantares de Dzitbalché*. Campeche: H.Ayuntamiento de Calkini, 1984.

Bateson, Gregory, *Steps to an Ecology of Mind*. Ballentine Books, 1972.

Baudelaire, Charles, *The Essence of Laughter and Other Essays, Journals, and Letters*. New York: Meridan Books, 1956.

Baylor, Byrd, *And It Is Still That Way, Legends told by Arizona Indian Children*. El Paso, TX: Cinco Puntos Press, 1998.

Becker, Ernest, *The Structure of Evil*. Free Press, 1976.

Berlin, Heinrich, Gonzalo de Balsalobre, and Diego de Hevia y Valdés, *Idolatría y superstición entre los indios de Oaxaca*. Ediciones Toledo, 1988.

Bierhorst, John, translator, *Cantares Mexicanos: Songs of the Aztecs*. Stanford University Press, 1985.

Blaffer, Sarah C., *The Black-Man of Zinacantán: A Central American Legend*. The Texas Pan American Series. Austin: University of Texas Press, 1972.

Bleibtreu, John N., *The Parable of the Beast*. Macmillan Company, 1968.

Bricker, Victoria, *Ritual Humor in Highland Chiapas*. Austin: University of Texas Press, 1973.

Bricker, Victoria, *The Indian Christ, the Indian King: The Historical Substrate of Maya Myth and Ritual*. Austin: University of Texas Press, 1981.

Brotherston, Gordon, *Painted books from Mexico: Codices in UK Collections and the World They Represent.* London: British Museum Press, 1995.

Brown, Penelope, *Language, Interaction, and Sex Roles in a Mayan Community: a Study of Politeness and the Position of Women.* Unpublished PhD dissertation. Berkeley: University of California, 1979. (Available through University Microfilms, Ann Arbor.)

Buitrago Ortiz, Carlos and Jessica Santos López, *Migración y mujeres indígenas hacia San Cristóbal de las Casas, Chiapas: un acercamiento etnográfico y cualitativo.* San Juan, PR: Universidad de Puerto Rico, 2004.

Burns, Allan Francisco, *Una epoca de milagros, literatura oral del maya yucateco.* Ediciones de la Universidad Autónoma de Yucatán, 1995.

Cantos Pieles-Rojas. Barcelona: José J. de Olañeta, 1983.

Cardenal, Ernesto, *Antología de poesía primitiva.* Madrid: Alianza, 1979.

Castellanos, Rosario, *Balun Canan.* Fondo de la Cultura Económica, 2007.

Castaneda, Carlos, *Journey to Ixtlan: Lessons of Don Juan.* Simon & Schuster, 1974.

Castiglioni, Arturo, *Encantamiento y mágia.* Fondo de la Cultura Económica, 2003.

Cocom Pech, Jorge, *Muk'ult'an in Nool.* UNAM, 2001.

Coe, Michael D, *The Maya, Ancient Peoples and Places.* Thames & Hudson, 2005.

Coe, Michael D, *Breaking the Maya Code.* Thames & Hudson, 1999.

Correa, Gustavo, "El espíritu del mal en Guatemala," in *Nativism and Syncretism.* Middle American Research Institute, Tulane University, 1960.

Cuevas Cob, Briceida, *Je' Bix K'iin(Como el sol).* Letras Mayas Contemporáneas, Instituto Nacional Indigenista, 1998.

Cuevas Cob, Briceida, *U yok'ol auat pek' ti u kuxtal pek' (El quejido del perro en su existeni*ca). Nave de papel, 1998.

Díaz de Castillo, Bernal, *The Conquest of New Spain.* Penguin Classics, 1963.

Dumestre, Gérard, *Palabras de África.* Barcelona: Ediciones Grupo Zeta, 1996.

Eber, Christine, *Women and Alcohol in a Highland Maya Town: Water of Hope, Water of Sorrow.* Austin: University of Texas Press, 2000.

Eber, Christine, *Seeking Justice, Valuing Community: Two women's paths in the wake of the Zapatista Rebellion.* Michigan State University, 1998.

El libro de los libros de Chilam Balam. Mexico: Fondo de Cultura Económica, 1998.

Farb, Peter, *Man's Rise to Civilization as Shown by the Indians of North America from Primeval Times to the Coming of the Industrial State.* New York: E. P. Dutton and Co. Inc., 1968.

Florescano, Enrique, *Memoria Indígena.* Mexico: Taurus, 1999.

Foster, George, "Nagualism in Mexico and Guatemala," in *Acta Americana* II, 1944.

Frazer, James G., *La rama dorada*. Mexico: Fondo de Cultura Económica 1993.

Frobenius, Leo, *The Childhood of Man: A Popular Account of the Lives, Customs and Thoughts of the Primitive Races*. Meridian Books, 1960.

García de León, Antonio, *Los elementos del Tzotzil colonial y moderno*, Centro de Estudios Mayas, Cuaderno 7. Mexico: Universidad Nacional Autónoma de Mexico, 1971.

Garcia Lorca, Federico, *Cantares populares*. Leer-e, 2007.

Garcia Quintanilla, Alejandra, *El dilema de Ah Kimsah K'ax, 'el que mata al monte': significados del monte entre los mayas milperos de Yucatán*. Mesoamerica, No. 39, Vol.21, 2000.

Garibay K., Ángel María (Garibay Kintana), *La literaturea de los aztecas*. Joaquín Mortiz Editorial, 1986.

Garibay K., Ángel María (Garibay Kintana), *Poesía indígena de la altiplanicie, divulgación literaria / Selección, versión, introducción y notas*. Mexico: Universidad Nacional Autónoma de Mexico, 1972.

Garibay K., Ángel María (Garibay Kintana), *Poesía náhuatl: Paleografía, versión, introd. y notas explicativas*, Mexico: Universidad Nacional Autónoma de Mexico, 1965.

Gomez-Peña, Guillermo, *Codex Espangliensis: from Columbus to the Border Patrol*. San Francisco: City Lights Books, 2001.

Gómez Ramírez, Martin, *Ofrenda de los ancestros en Oxchuc*. Chiapas: Instituto Chiapaneco de Cultura, 1988.

Gossen, Gary H., *Chamulas in the World of the Sun: Time and Space in a Maya Oral Tradition*. Waveland Press, 1984.

Gregorio Regino, Juan, *Ngata'ara stse (Que siga lloviendo)*. Mexico, 1999.

Guadarrama López, Fausto (compilador) *Amanecer / Ra jyasu: Antología de poesía mazahua contemporánea*. Editorial Praxis, 1999.

Guiteras Holmes, Calixta, *Cancuc: Etnografía de un pueblo tzeltal de los Altos de Chiapas, 1944*. Instituto Chiapaneco de Cultura. Mexico, 2003.

Guiteras Holmes, Calixta, "La magia en la crisis del embarazo y parto en los actuales grupos mayences de Chiapas," en *Estudios de Cultura Maya, Vol. 1*. Mexico: Universidad Nacional Autónoma de Mexico, 1961.

Guiteras Holmes, Calixta, *Perils of the Soul: The World View of a Tzotzil Indian*. The Free Press, 1962.

Haviland, John Beard, *Sk'op sotz'leb: El Tzotzil de San Lorenzo Zinacantán*. Mexico: Universidad Nacional Autónoma de Mexico, 1981.

Holland, William, *Medicina Maya en los Altos de Chiapas: Un estudio del cambio socio-cultural*. Mexico: Instituto Nacional Indigenista, 1963.

Holland, William, *Contemporary Tzotzil Cosmological Concepts as a Basis for Interpreting Prehistoric Maya Civilization*. Mexico: Instituto Nacional de Antropología e Historia, 1962.

Huxley, Aldous, *Prácticas religiosas en meseoamérica*. Guatemala: Ministerio de Educación, 1965.

Imberton Deneke, Gracia María, *La vergüenza. Enfermedad y conflicto en una comunidad chol.* Mexico: Universidad Nacional Autónoma de Mexico, 2002.

Jacobson, Marcey, *The Burden of Time, photographs from the Highlands of Chiapas.* Palo Alto: Stanford University Press, 2001.

Jossarand, J. Kathyryn, and Karen Dakin, eds, *Smoke and Mist: Mesoamerian Studies in Memory of Thelma D. Sullivan.* Oxford: British Archaeological Reports, International Series, 1988.

Jung, Carl G., *Man and His Symbols.* Dell, 1968.

Knab, Dr. T.J. (Editor), and Thelma D. Sullivan, (Translator), *A Scattering of Jades. Stories, Poems and Prayers of the Aztecs.* Simon & Schuster, 1994.

Köhler, Ulrich, *Chonbilal Ch'ulelal-Alma Vendia.* Mexico: Universidad Nacional Autónoma de Mexico, 1997.

Koyaso Panchin, Marian, *Loíl yuún Kuskat, (Cuento sobre Cuscat).* Taller Tzotzil INARAMAC, 1988.

Landa, Fray Diego de, *Relación de las cosas de Yucatán.* Producción Editorial Dante, S.A., 1997.

Leander, Brigitta, *In xochitl in cuicatl: Flor y canto, la poesía de los aztecas.* Mexico: Instituto Nacional Indigenista, 1980.

Laughlin, Robert M., *The Flowering of Man, A Tzotzil Botany of Zinacantán.* Washington D.C.: Smithsonian Institution Press, Smithsonian Contributions to Anthropology #35, 1993.

Laughlin, Robert M., *The Great Tzotzil Dictionary of San Lorenzo Zinacantán.* Washington D.C.: Smithsonian Institution Press, Smithsonian Contributions to Anthropology #19, 1975.

Laughlin, Robert M., *Mayan Tales and Dreams from Zinacantán: Dreams and Stories from the People of the Bat.* Washington D.C.: Smithsonian Institution Press, 1988.

Laughlin, Robert M., *Of Cabbages and Kings, Tales from Zinacantán.* Washington D.C.: Smithsonian Institution Press, Smithsonian Contributions to Anthropology #23, 1977.

Laughlin, Robert M., *Of Shoes and Ships and Sealing Wax, Sundries from Zinacantán.* Washington D.C.: Smithsonian Institution Press, Smithsonian Contributions to Anthropology #25, 1980.

Laughlin, Robert M., *Of Wonders Wild and New: Dreams from Zinacantán.* Washington D.C.: Smithsonian Institution Press, Smithsonian Contributions to Anthropology #22, 1988.

Laughlin, Robert M., *Zinacantán: Canto y sueño.* Instituto Nacional Indigenista, 1992.

Lara Figueroa, Celso Al, *Viejas consejas: Sobre Santos milagrosos y señores de los cerros.* Artimis-Edinter, 1995.

Leirana Alcocer, Silvia Cristina, *Conjurando el silencio.* Mérida, Yucatán: Instituto de Cultura de Yucatán, 2005.

Lenkersdorf, Carlos, *Cosmovisión Maya.* Mexico: Centro de Estudios Antropológicos, 2003.

Lenkersdorf, Carlos, *Relatos de los tojolabales, mayas de los Altos de Chiapas en Mexico.* Indiana, Berlin, 1975.

León-Portilla, Miguel, *Códices, los antiguos libros del nuevo mundo.* Mexico: Aguilar, 2003.

León-Portilla, Miguel, *La filosofía nahuatl: estudiada en sus fuentes*. Mexico: Universidad Nacional Autónoma de Mexico, 1956.

León-Portilla, Miguel, *Trece poetas del mundo azteca*. Mexico: Universidad Nacional Autónoma de Mexico, 1978.

López-Austin, Alfredo, *Tamoanchan Y Tlalocan (Seccion De Obras De Antropologia)*. Fondo de Cultura Económica, 1998.

Luxton, Richard and Balam, Pablo, *Sueño del camino maya*. Fondo de Cultura Económica, 1986.

Mackenzie, Donald A., *Pre-Colombian America: Myths and Legends*. New York: Senate, 1996.

Malinowski, Bronislaw, *Magic, Science and Religión*. Doubleday Anchor, 1954.

Martínez Fure, Rogelio, *Poesía Anónima Africana*. Cuba: Editorial Arte y Literatura, 1985.

Miller, Mary and Karl Taube, *An Illustrated Dictionary of the Gods and Symbols of Ancient Mexico and the Maya*. Thames and Hudson, 1993.

Montejo, Victor Dionicio, *El Kanil Man of Lightning*. Signal Books, 1982.

Montemayor, Carlos, *"Loíl maxil yu'un Chyapa,"* Voces de Chiapas. Unidad de Esciritores Mayas-Zoques, 1996.

Morales Bermúdez, Jesús, *On o t'ian, antigual palabra narrativa indígena Ch'ol*. Universiad Autonoma Metropolitana, Unidad Azcapotzalco,1985.

Morris, Walter F., *Living Maya*. New York: Harry N. Abrams, Inc., 2000.

Moscoso Pastrana, Prudencio, *Las cabezas rodantes del mal: brujería y nahualismo en los altos de Chiapas*. Gobierno del Estado de Chiapas, 1991.

Nash, June, *Bajo la mirada de los antepasados: creencias y comportamiento en una comunidad maya*. Mexico: Instituto Indigenista Americano, 1975.

Navarrete, Carlos, *Tres poemas zoques*. Rodrigo Nuñez Editories 1984.

Noh Tzec, Waldemar, *Noj Bálam (El Grande Jaguar)*. Instituto Nacional Indigenista, 1998.

Olivera Bustamante, Mercedes, (ed.) *De sumisiones, cambios, y rebeldías: mujeres indígenas de Chiapas*. Tuxtla Gutiérrez, Chiapas: Universidad de Ciencias y Artes Chiapas, 2004.

Ochaia, Kazuyasu, *Cuando los santos vienen marchando: rituales públicos intercomunitarios Tzotziles*. Mexico: Universidad Autónoma de Chiapas, 1985.

Ortega y Gasset, José, *Cantos y cuentos del antiguo Egipto*. Mexico: Costa-Amoc Editores, 1981.

Past, Burstein, Wasserstrom, *Slo'il jchiltaktik, Cuatro Vidas Tzotziles*. Mexico: Editorial Fray Bartolome de las Casas, 1978.

Past, Ámbar, *Bon Tintes Naturales*. Mexico: Taller Leñateros, 1980.

Past, Ámbar, *Conjuros y ebriedades, cantos de mujeres mayas*. Mexico: Taller Leñateros, 1998.

Past, Ámbar, *Incantations by Maya Women*. Mexico: Taller Leñateros, 2005.

Paz, Octavio, *Versiones y Diversiones*. Joaquín Mortiz, 1974.

Pellizzi, Francesco, "Misioneros y Cargos: Notas sobre Identidad y Aculturación en los Altos de Chiapas," *América Indígena*, Vol. XLII. Mexico: Instituto Indigenista Interamericano, 1982.

Peñalosa, Fernando, *The Mayan Folktale: An Introduction*. Yax te' Press, 1996.

Pérez López, Enrique, *Yalan Bek'et. Bájate Carne*. Mexico: Universidad Nacional Autónoma de Mexico, 1995.

Pérez Pérez, Ánselmo, Juan de la Torre López, Domingo Heredia Hernández, Isabel Juárez Espinosa, and Sebastian Ramírez Intzin, *Los antiguos comerciantes zinacantecos Vo'ne jchonolajetik ta tzinakanta*. Secretaría de Educación y Cultura del Estado de Chiapas, 1984.

Pitt-Rivers, Julian, "Spiritual Power in Central America: The Naguals of Chiapas," *Witchcraft Accusations and Confessions*, Mary Douglas (ed.). Tavistock Publications, 1970.

Pitarch, Pedro, *Ch'ulel: una etnografía de las almas Tzeltales*. Mexico: Fondo de Cultura Económica, 1996.

Pound, Ezra and Stock, Noel, *Love Poems of Ancient Egypt*. New Directions, 1978.

Pozas, Ricardo, *Chamula, un pueblo indio de los altos de Chiapas*. Mexico: Memorias del Instituto Nacional Indigenista, Vol. 8, 1959.

Pozas, Ricardo, *Juan Pérez Jolote: biografía de un Tzotzil*. 1948.

Rabinal-Achi, Ballet-drama de los indios quichés de Guatemala, traducción y prólogo de Luis Cardoza y Aragón. Guatemala, 1971.

Redfield, Robert and Alfonso Villa Rojas, *Chan Kom, A Maya Village*. Washington, D.C.: Carnegie Institution of America, 1934.

Róheim, Géza, *Magic and Schizophrenia*. Bloomington: Indiana University Press, 1970.

Róheim, Géza, *The Gates of the Dream*. New York: International Universities Press, Inc, 1973.

Rosenbaum, Brenda, *With Our Heads Bowed: The Dynamics of Gender in a Maya Community*. Institute for Mesoamerican Studies, 1993.

Rothenberg, Jerome, *Shaking the Pumpkin, Traditional Poetry of the Indian North Americas*. Albuquerque: University of New Mexico Press, 1992.

Rothenberg, Jerome, *Technicians of the Sacred: A Range of Poetries from Africa, America, Asia, and Oceania*. New York: Doubleday & Co., Inc., 1968.

Rovira, Guiomar, *Mujeres de maiz: la voz de las indígenas de Chiapas y la rebelion zapatista*. Mexico: Ediciones Era, 1997.

Roys, Ralph L. (ed), *Ritual of the Bacabs: A Book of Maya Incantations*. Norman: University of Oklahoma Press, 1965.

Rus, Diane, *Mujeres de tierra fría. Conversaciones con las coletas*. Universidad de Ciencias y Artes del Estado de Chiapas, Tuxtla Gutiérrez, 1998.

Rus, Jan, "Whose Caste War? Indians, Ladinos, and the Chiapas 'Caste War' of 1869," *Spaniards and Indians in Southeastern Mesoamerica: Essays on the History of Ethnic Relations*. Lincoln, NE., University of Nebraska Press, 1983.

Rus, Jan and Diane, coordinators, *Abtel ta pinka*. Taller Tzotzil, INAREMAC, 1986.

Ruz, Alberto Lhuillier, *La civilización de los antiguos mayas*. Fondo de la Cultura Económica, 1997.

Ruz, Mario Humberto, *Historias domésticas: tradición oral en la Sierra Madre de Chiapas*. Universidad Autónoma de Chiapas, 1991.

Sahagún, Fray Bernardino de, *Historia general de las cosas de Nueva España*. Editorial Porrua,1969.

Sahagún, Fray Bernardino de, *Oraciones, Adagios, Adivinanzas y metáforas: Libro sexto del Códice Florentino*. Universidad Nacional Autónoma de Mexico, 1995.

Saler, Benson, "Nagual, Witch, and Sorcerer in a Quiché Village," *Ethnology*, 3. University of Pittsburgh, 1964.

Sarris, Greg, *Mabel McKay: Weaving the Dream*. University of California Press, 1994.

Schele, Linda and David Freidel, *A Forest of Kings: The Untold Story of the Ancient Maya*. William Morrow, 1990.

Sodi M, Demetrio, *La literatura de los mayas*. Joaquin Mortiz, 1964.

Sontag, Susan, *Regarding the Pain of Others*. Picador, 2003.

Speed, Shannon, R. Aída Hernández Castillo, and Lynn M. Stephen (ed.) *Dissident Women: Gender and Cultural Politics in Chiapas*. Austin: University of Texas Press, 2006.

Swann, Brian (editor), *Native American Songs and Poems, an Anthology*. Dover Publications, 1996.

Taube, Karl, *Aztec and Maya Myths*. Austin: University of Texas Press, 1993.

Tedlock, Barbara, *Time and the Highland Maya*. Albuquerque: University of New Mexico Press, 1985.

Tozzer, Alfred M., *A Comparative Study of the Mayas and the Lacandones*. London: The Macmillan Company, 1907.

Wilson, Carter, *Crazy February: Death and Life in the Mayan Highlands of Mexico*. University of California Press, 1974.

Wilson, Carter, *A Green Tree and a Dry Tree*. Macmillan, 1972.

Vogel, Virgil J., *American Indian Medicine*. Norman: University of Oklahoma Press, 1990.

Vos, Jan de, *La paz de Dios y del rey. La conquista de la Selva Lacandona por los españoles*. Mexico: Fonapas, 1980.

Walker, Gayle and Suárez, Kiki, *Every Woman is a World: Interviews with Women of Chiapas*. Austin: University of Texas Press, 2008

Ximenez, Francisco, *Historia de la Provincia de San Vicente de Chiapas y Guatemala de la Orden de Predicadores*. Editorial Sociedad de Geografía e Historia de Guatemala, 1929.

Zaid, Gabriel, *Omnibus de la poesía mexicana*. Siglo XXI Editores, 1972.